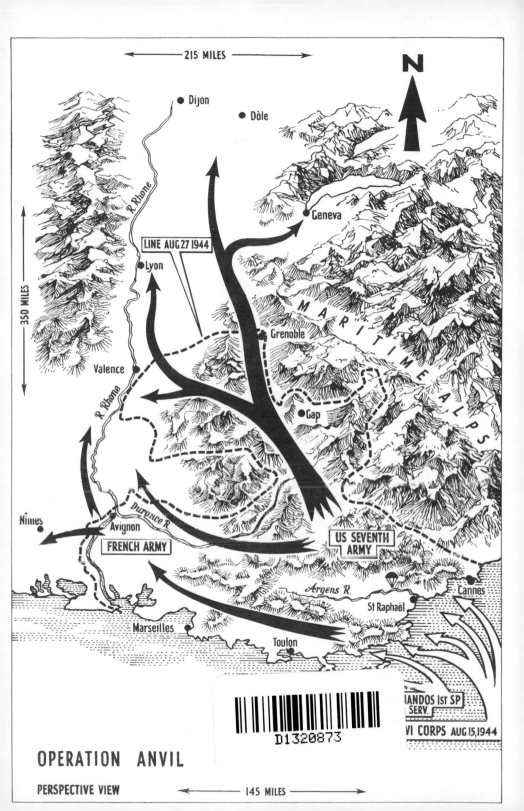

OPERATION ANVIL

PERSPECTIVE VIEW

Destination
Berchtesgaden

Destination Berchtesgaden

The Story of the United States
Seventh Army in World War II

JOHN FRAYN TURNER
&
ROBERT JACKSON

LONDON
IAN ALLAN LTD

First published 1975

ISBN 0 7110 0603 2-99/74

Published by Ian Allan Ltd, Shepperton, Surrey
and printed in the United Kingdom by
The Garden City Press Limited, Letchworth, Herts.

I

The storm came out of the west, sweeping across the length of the Mediterranean from the Straits of Gibraltar to lash the normally-placid seas into a tumult. Around the rocky coast of Sicily, German and Italian sentries gazed at clouds that raced across the evening sky and wondered if the gale would last long enough to bring a temporary respite from the Allied bombers, which for weeks now had been pounding the island's defences by day or night.

It was July 9th, 1943, and after three and a half bitter years the tide of war was at last beginning to turn against the Axis. In the Atlantic, hunter-killer task forces and aircraft combined to hound the U-boat wolfpacks to their deaths; on the Eastern Front, the German Sixth Army had been annihilated in the rubble of Stalingrad, and the Russians were massing their forces for an offensive in the Kursk salient; the once-proud Afrika Korps, trapped between the British Eighth Army and American forces, had fought its last battle in Tunisia; and the heart of Germany was burning under the holocaust of the Anglo-American strategic bombing offensive. The Axis leaders knew now beyond all doubt that it was only a question of time before the Allies attempted to gain a foothold on the mainland of Europe; what they did not know yet was where the blow would fall.

On July 9th, the German and Italian garrisons on Sicily had no way of knowing that they were the target for the first Allied invasion of Europe, or that the blow was only hours from being struck. The decision to attack Sicily had, in fact, been reached only after considerable argument and discussion between the British and Americans. At the end of 1942, the British, foreseeing the elimination of the Axis forces from North Africa following the successful Allied landings there in November, envisaged exploiting this victory by pushing across the Mediterranean. They wanted to land in Sicily, Sardinia, the Italian mainland or southern France; they also

5

believed that such an action might persuade Turkey to enter the war on the side of the Allies. The Americans, on the other hand, wanted to build up their forces in Britain to launch a direct invasion across the Channel in 1943; they had no desire to continue the offensive in the Mediterranean, other than to step up the strategic bombing of Italy to lower Italian morale.

It was this divergence of opinion that led to an Allied summit conference at Casablanca in January, 1943, during which President Roosevelt, Prime Minister Winston Churchill and their advisers met to thrash out a plan of campaign following the Allied victory in North Africa. The Americans, who now tended to the viewpoint that the North African campaign—with its considerable drain on Allied resources—would make a cross-Channel invasion in 1943 impossible in any case, finally agreed to an invasion of Sicily. At a later conference, held in Washington in May, 1943, the Allied leaders agreed that they would consider operations beyond Sicily, in other words an invasion of Italy, only insofar as they were likely to expedite and facilitate a thrust across the Channel into north-west Europe.

In the end a form of compromise was reached; it was decided to launch a cross-Channel invasion in May, 1944, in the meantime attempting to knock Italy out of the war by using the forces available in the Mediterranean Theatre—though seven of these divisions were to be transferred to England by November, 1943.

For the invasion of Sicily, the Combined Chiefs of Staff envisaged two task forces, one British and the other American. To command the British ground forces the Supreme Allied Commander, General Eisenhower, nominated General Sir Bernard Law Montgomery, who had led the Eighth Army in the 1,500 mile pursuit of the Afrika Korps from Egypt to Tunisia; while the Americans were to be commanded by Major-General George S. Patton, Jr, who had led the Western Task Force in the invasion of North Africa, the II Corps in Tunisia, and who was now to lead the newly created United States Seventh Army in Sicily. Overall command of the Allied ground forces rested on the shoulders of General Sir Harold R. L. G. Alexander, while Admiral Sir Andrew B. Cunningham led the naval forces and Air-Chief-Marshal Sir Arthur Tedder the Air Forces.

Planning for the invasion continued throughout the spring of 1943. The Combined Chiefs recommended two simultaneous assaults, one near Palermo and the other near Catania; this would permit the seizure of two of the island's major ports and facilitate the capture of most airfields; the two spearheads could then drive on Messina along the island's northern and eastern shores. There were, however, certain disadvantages to this idea; for one thing the two separate forces would be unable to support each other directly, and for another they would need far greater numbers of troops

6

and shipping to carry out their assault. Alexander, on the other hand, favoured a concentrated assault by both task forces against the south-east coast of Sicily; however, his planners pointed out that the ports in this area would be inadequate to support the large weight of men and material required for the landing. The planners recommended two simultaneous assaults, one by the British in the south-east, the other by the Americans in the west; this followed roughly the lines laid down by the Combined Chiefs, but Montgomery objected on the grounds that a landing in the south-east would mean the stretching of his forces around 100 miles of coast between Gela and Catania to the point where they would be vulnerable to counter-attack. He, like Alexander, favoured a concentrated assault—but on the east coast.

To try to resolve these and other arguments, Eisenhower called a conference of the military commanders in Algiers on April 29th. This time, an officer representing Montgomery submitted a new plan which envisaged an Anglo-American assault in the south-east, with the British landing along the Gulf of Noto and the Americans going ashore on both sides of the Pachino Peninsula. On May 2nd, the invasion plan was finalised; the British would strike on the eastern coast from the Pachino Peninsula to Syracuse, the Americans along the Gulf of Gela from Licata to the Pachino Peninsula.

The invasion force assembled in North Africa during May and June. The British Eighth Army would open its assault with glider troops, who were to capture Ponte Grande and open the road to the taking of Syracuse; they were also, if possible, to capture some coastal batteries and a seaplane base. Another major coastal battery at Cape Murro di Porco, south of Syracuse, was to be eliminated by commandos as a prelude to the main attack.

Lieutenant-General Sir Miles Dempsey's XIII Corps was to put ashore the 5th Division, which would take Cassibile before turning north towards Syracuse; the Corps's left flank would be protected by the 59th Division, which was to capture Avola. The XXX Corps, under Lieutenant-General Sir Oliver Leese, was to send in the 231st Infantry Brigade Group, the 51st Division and the 1st Canadian Division against the Pachino Peninsula; after linking up with the Americans at Ragusa, this force was to push on to Palazzolo and Vizzini, extending northwards along the east coast to allow Dempsey to move a major part of his strength against Augusta and Catania.

The assault by Patton's Seventh Army was to begin with the dropping of elements of the 82nd Airborne Division—the 505th Parachute Regiment and the 3rd Battalion of the 504th—on Piano Lupo, approximately in the centre of the American front and several miles inland from Gela. The task of the paratroops was to cut off the enemy approaches to the beaches during the early landing phase of the invasion, when the seaborne troops were extremely vulnerable to counter-attack. The seaborne invasion was to take the form of a three-pronged thrust; on the right the 45th Division was to go ashore near the fishing village of Scoglitti and the 1st Division at Gela, both under the command of Major-General Omar N. Bradley's II Corps, while on the left the 3rd Division would land at Licata.

Opposing the Allied forces, the enemy garrison on Sicily numbered some 200,000 Italians and 30,000 Germans. The Italian XVI Corps, under Generale-di-Corpo-d'Armata Caeto Rossi, was responsible for the defence of the eastern half of the island with the Napoli and Livorno Divisions. The XII Corps under Generale-di-Corpo-d'Armata Francesco Zingales defended the western half with the Aosta and Assietta Divisions. The German contribution consisted of the 15th Panzer Grenadier Division, which was split into three task forces and concentrated in the west, while the Hermann Göring Division was split into two combat teams which were located in the south and east. The Sicilian defences were commanded by Generale-d'Armata Alfredo Guzzoni, who had been called out of retirement to take over the post.

In June, 1943, Allied forces occupied the islands of Lampedusa and Pantelleria, which fell with hardly a shot in the wake of a massive air bombardment. After this reverse, Guzzoni was under no illusion about the Allies's next target. He also knew that unless the Germans despatched huge reinforcements to Sicily, the outcome of such an invasion would be a foregone conclusion. And by the end of the first week in July, no reinforcements had yet materialised.

The time and date for the invasion had been selected by Eisenhower in May, at the close of the Tunisian campaign. The choice depended to a great extent on the phase of the moon, for whereas the naval forces needed darkness to bring in their convoys towards the objectives, the airborne forces required a certain amount of light to carry out their landings. The night of July 9th satisfied these demands; the airborne forces were scheduled to go in shortly after midnight and the seaborne forces would hit the beaches at 0245 on the 10th.

The ships of the invasion force—3,500 vessels of all types, organised into two task forces—sailed from various North African ports and reached their rendezvous points on the morning of July 9th, just as the wind began to increase, reaching speeds of up to 40mph. Thousands of troops, especially those huddled in the landing craft, went through the violent misery of sea-sickness as the vessels wallowed and rolled in waves, the crests of which reached 20-30ft. During the afternoon, as the armada turned north to make its final approach, the swell struck a broadside on; cargoes shifted and many of the vessels lost station. For a time, there was a possibility that the whole operation might have to be postponed for twenty-four hours. Then, as the ships passed Malta, the wind dropped and the decision was taken to go ahead.

At 1930, as the convoys split up and headed for their respective targets, Allied bombers, battling through the high wind, launched heavy attacks on Sicilian targets in the vicinity of the beachheads. Meanwhile, the aircraft towing the British gliderborne troops were forming up over the Tunisian coast. Behind them, on the North African airfields, the men of the 82nd Airborne filed aboard their fleet of C-47s, waiting their turn to go.

At 2210, the first wave of British gliders swept down towards their objectives—but this phase of the operation was already beginning to go badly amiss. Of the 115 gliders released, over half—hopelessly lost in the gale and darkness—fell into the sea. Only 54 landed in Sicily, and of these only a dozen were anywhere near their targets. Instead of 1,000 British airborne troops, a mere 100 managed to assemble as planned; these set out towards their first objective, a bridge south of Syracuse.

Two hours later, the American fleet of 222 C-47s, carrying 3,400 paratroops, departed from North Africa and set course over the Mediterranean. This force, too, soon ran into trouble; many of the pilots, inexperienced in night flying, failed to keep station, with the result that scattered groups of transport aircraft converged on Sicily from all directions. Some of the C-47s turned back; those which succeeded in making landfalls dropped their paratroops all over southern Sicily. Very few of the men had any real idea of their location; the force commander, Brigadier-General James Gavin, was for a time not convinced that they had been dropped in Sicily at all. Nevertheless, the paratroops did what they could to salvage some order out of the general chaos; 200 of them succeeded in occupying their primary objective, some high ground at Piano Lupo, while the others roamed across the countryside in small groups, overrunning pillboxes, seizing bridges and crossroads and cutting communications. It was small wonder that, at 0100, General Guzzoni received the first confused reports that the whole of southern Sicily had been invaded by "massive airborne forces".

At 0245, the seaborne landings began. While Montgomery's forces headed inshore for a successful assault in the Syracuse and Cape Passero sectors, the assault troops of the Seventh Army's sub-task forces churned through the heavy swell towards the Gela beaches. The American invasion covered a 57 mile front. Sub-task force Cent, comprising the 45th Division, struck for the shore on the right flank, covering the beaches from Scoglitti

9

to Fiume Agata, 10 miles south-east of Gela; Dime Force, consisting of the 1st Division minus the 18th Regimental Combat Team, headed in between Fiume Agata and Gela, with a Ranger Force on its left moving in for a frontal assault on Gela; while Joss Force, the 3rd Infantry Division supported by elements of the 2nd Armoured Division, moved in to launch their attack on either side of Gela.

Unlike the British landings, which were somewhat sheltered from the full strength of the westerly gale, the Seventh Army's landings at Gela proved a difficult task. One of the convoys, carrying the 45th Division, was seriously behind schedule and its landing had to be postponed one hour; the 1st and 3rd Divisions began their assaults more or less on time, but the waves of landing craft had a hard time battling their way to shore through the heavy swell. As they smashed through the breakers, they encountered heavy fire at first, but this was soon eliminated by salvoes from the Allied warships lying offshore. The infantry encountered only sporadic resistance as they pushed their way up the beaches, cautiously prodding the bushes around the sand dunes with bayonets. Here and there they took a prisoner as they drove on into the hills beyond, heading for the vital high ground at Piano Lupo and its road junction. No one was as yet aware that this objective had not been captured by the paratroops, as planned.

It was at Piano Lupo that General Guzzoni ordered his forces to concentrate for an attack on the Seventh Army's beachhead; there was, however, a certain amount of confusion and delay as the enemy columns ran into road-blocks thrown up by the groups of American paratroops. The first enemy unit to approach Piano Lupo, Mobile Group E, was halted by a force of 100 paratroops, who pinned down the leading Italian elements with highly accurate fire until they were forced to pull back under a rain of shells. The Italian column was then spotted by reconnaissance patrols from the Gela beachhead, who called down naval gunfire on it. Twenty Italian tanks attempted to break through, but two of these were knocked out by the Americans coming up from the beaches and the remainder turned back under a growing weight of naval shell-fire. The bulk of Mobile Column E subsequently took up new positions in the foothills north of Gela, leaving a small force of infantry occupying the crossroads at Piano Lupo. This was later wiped out by the paratroops, who afterwards linked up with units from the beaches.

Meanwhile, the Livorno Division launched a two-pronged attack against Gela from the north-west, preceded by twenty tanks. Several of these were knocked out by fire from the warships, but the rest penetrated Gela. They were hotly engaged by US Rangers, who hunted them with rocket launchers and hand grenades through the narrow streets. After thirty minutes, the surviving tanks pulled out along the road to Butera. Some time later, 600 infantry of the Livorno Division also advanced on Gela, but they were decimated by American small-arms and mortar fire and the attack shrivelled up before reaching the town. On the other side of Gela, an advance by tanks and infantry of Major-General Paul Conrath's Hermann Göring Division was also halted by heavy naval gunfire.

Sporadic fighting continued throughout the American sectors during the rest of the day, but by nightfall the Seventh Army was in firm control of Licata, Gela and Scoglitti. The British forces were also securely ashore in the east, having given the Napoli Division a severe mauling, and the unloading of supplies and equipment went ahead smoothly in all sectors despite occasional bombing by enemy aircraft.

During the night of July 10th/11th, General Guzzoni and his staff laid plans to launch a strong counter-offensive against the beachheads. On learning that Syracuse had fallen, his main concern was to prevent the British from breaking through to the Catania Plain, over which they could drive towards Messina. He therefore ordered the Livorno and Hermann Göring Divisions to launch a concerted attack on Gela; as soon as this showed signs of success, the Germans were to be switched eastwards to join combat with the British. After capturing Gela, the Livorno Division was then to move westwards on Licata.

The Livorno Division opened its attack at 0615 on July 11th, in conjunction with an air attack on the American beachhead, but it was not long before the Italian advance was halted by naval shell-fire. The advance by the Hermann Göring Division met with some initial success, overrunning a few American forward positions. The German advance was harried by groups of paratroops led by Brigadier General Gavin, but Conrath was nevertheless able to concentrate the bulk of his forces against Gela. The Livorno Division, meanwhile, had resumed its attack against the US 1st Division on the western side of Gela, and the Americans poured all their available firepower into the defence of this sector. General Patton, observing the battle from a command post in Gela, shouted to American troops and exhorted them to "kill every one of the Goddam bastards".

The defenders carried out Patton's command almost to the letter. From the warships offshore, a hurricane of 6in shells slammed into the advancing Italians, scything great gaps in their ranks. As the advance wavered, units of the 1st Division and the US Rangers moved forward through the smoke, engaging the dazed Italians in close-range combat. They took 400 prisoners as the Livorno Division broke, leaving mounds of dead on the battlefield. For the time being, the Livorno was shattered as an effective fighting force.

On the other flank, the Hermann Göring Division's tanks forged ahead through a holocaust of shell-bursts. For a time it looked as though the Germans were on the point of winning a clear-cut victory; the leading tanks broke through to within 2,000 yards of the shore and opened up an intense fire on the American landing craft and supply dumps. At this point, the armour's advance was halted by naval gunfire; while US infantry, Rangers and Engineers, hastily formed a firing-line and picked off the tanks's supporting troops. Unable to progress in the teeth of the barrage, the Panzers halted in confusion at the edge of the coastal road, and as they piled up naval shells wrought more havoc among them. At 1400, Conrath decided to abandon his attack and the tanks pulled back, leaving sixteen of their number burning on the battlefield. During the late afternoon, the Hermann Göring Division assembled in the foothills south of Niscemi as a preliminary to a further withdrawal to Caltagirone.

By the end of D-plus-1, the Seventh Army, as well as withstanding the determined enemy counter-strokes on its centre, had managed to extend its beachhead inland on both left and right flanks. American losses from the beginning of the invasion had by then totalled 175 killed, 2,594 missing and 665 wounded. The GIs had taken 8,655 prisoners and knocked out more than 40 enemy tanks. On the right, the 45th Division had taken Comiso and its neighbouring airfield, capturing 125 German aircraft, 200,000 gallons of fuel and 500 bombs. One company of the 45th had also entered Ragusa, capturing the mayor and several other key officials and seizing the telephone switchboard. All Seventh Army units were now in contact with each other; elements of the 2nd Armoured Division were ashore and in action on the left, and the unloading of equipment continued at a fast rate despite determined efforts by the enemy air forces to disrupt it. The Seventh Army's command ship, USS *Monrovia*, suffered a near-miss by 50ft during a high-level bombing attack from 12 Italian aircraft, and in the afternoon 30 Junkers 88s destroyed a Liberty ship loaded with ammunition, which went up with a terrific explosion.

During the night of July 11th/12th, the second lift of the 82nd Airborne Division—comprising 2,000 men under the command of Colonel Reuben H. Tucker—was scheduled for dropping over Sicily from 144 transport aircraft. Unfortunately, the first wave of C-47s arrived over the beachhead at the same time as a wave of enemy bombers, and in the ensuing chaos American antiaircraft batteries mistook the transports for enemy planes and opened up on them. Several aircraft were hit and crashed in the sea, together with their loads of paratroops; other pilots lost their bearings after taking evasive action and some paratroops landed as far away from the dropping zones as central Sicily. Many of them died in the mountains there. Still other paratroopers, jumping in panic from stricken aircraft, were swallowed up by the Mediterranean. Of the 144 aircraft that set out from Tunisia, 23 failed to return—6 of them shot down before they could drop their paratroops—and 37 were severely damaged.

At daybreak on July 12th, the enemy once more hurled armour and infantry at the American II Corps south of Niscemi. The 1st Division withstood this assault which proved to be the last attempt by the enemy to prevent the firm establishment of the American beachhead. During the morning, the 1st Division took Ponte Olivo airfield, inflicting still more punishment on the battered Livorno Division in the process; and on the extreme right of the Seventh Army sector, elements of the 45th Division in Ragusa linked up with the British Eighth Army. By the end of the day, the Seventh Army's foothold in Sicily extended from a depth of 8 miles at Gela to 15 miles on either flank.

Meanwhile, engineers had removed obstructions from the landing field west of Gela, and—acting quickly to disarm mines and delayed-action charges—had saved the runways of Ponte Olivo from destruction. Straggler control and traffic direction were organised in Gela, and the security of enemy ammunition dumps and abandoned headquarters assured. The advanced Seventh Army command post moved ashore from the USS *Monrovia* in mid-afternoon, establishing one echelon in a school building and another north of the town in a grove. The day's losses were down to 29 killed, 106 missing and 183 wounded, while the Americans had destroyed 43 enemy tanks and taken 4,206 prisoners. In the course of the day, one American LST was bombed and sunk.

The original idea had been to extend the beachheads until the enemy was driven back to a line where his long-range artillery could not reach the airfields at Ponte Olivo, Comiso and Biscari; so that these, together with the port and airfield at Licata, could be used by the Seventh Army. On July 13th, however, the 3rd Division was directed to carry on reconnoitring as far as Agrigento and to hold Canicatti. The major enemy effort appeared to be east and west of a general line from Caltagirone to Gela; elements of the Hermann Göring Division were in action in this area, but despite their presence all Seventh Army units continued to advance.

Now firmly entrenched on Sicily, the Seventh Army prepared to put captured airfields and communications into service. The airfield at Ponte Olivo, a glider strip north-west of Gela and a landing strip 2 miles east of the town were all ready to receive aircraft. A new airstrip was also completed at Licata, and the first Allied fighters landed there on July 13th.

This period, which saw the transition from assault to consolidation, presented its fair share of problems. No fewer than 2,033 more prisoners were taken on the 13th, bringing the total of captured enemy troops—mostly Italians—to such proportions that they began to give the Seventh Army a severe headache. Divisions were burdened with hundreds of prisoners and lacked the transport required to move them quickly to POW cages. Civilian medical problems also became acute. The Americans had to limit hospitalisation to grave cases.

Late that evening, a battle group of the Hermann Göring Division was reported 5 miles east of Niscemi. An American officer, captured by the Germans, later escaped and was able to confirm previous estimates that there were two German divisions on the island. Frustrated by the failure of their counter-attacks, the enemy now withdrew towards the Catania Plain and northwards beyond Caltagirone. The Americans swung their effort north-westwards; on II Corps's left the 1st Division took Niscemi and Mazzarino, while a general link-up occurred along the beachheads. There now existed a continuous beachhead across the whole of south-east Sicily, with both flanks anchored on the sea. The capture of Biscari airfield completed the series of initial tasks assigned to the Seventh Army.

D-plus-4 is therefore a good moment to pause and analyse the achievement thus far. Prisoners totalled 13,000, while the enemy had lost some 1,400 men killed or wounded. Most of the prisoners were being evacuated to North Africa as quickly as possible. Many of the Italians spoke bitterly of their German allies, whom they accused of sacrificing Italians to cover their own withdrawal. On at least one occasion, the Germans retreated ahead of the Italians and mined the roads as they went, trapping the Italians between the minefields and the advancing Americans.

The first major change in the composition and direction of the Seventh Army advance came on July 15th, when the time was ripe for a major drive west and north-west through the island. During the next two days, II Corps accordingly pivoted to swing the entire Seventh Army front round in readiness for this thrust towards the northern coast. The Seventh's total strength at this stage was 203,204 men.

The general German retreat was covered by armour, operating in units of up to sixteen tanks, but the US 1st Division swept aside all opposition to enter Barrafranca on July 16th. Although this was reckoned a quiet day, the capture of high ground north of Agrigento yielded a not insignificant haul of 4,000 Italian prisoners. That night and the next day, naval guns backed up the 3rd Division's advance on Agrigento as the Americans captured the town. Over 6,000 prisoners were taken in this action, bringing the total to 20,000.

The enemy withdrawal continued as the invasion entered its second week, and during the night of July 17th/18th contact was broken along the whole front, enabling the Allies to push on as planned. New orders were issued, detailing the mission of the Allied armies in Sicily. The British Eighth Army was to drive the enemy north and east into the Messina Peninsula; the general Seventh Army mission was to spearhead north and take Palermo, on the north-west coast. Things were beginning to move rapidly now.

Troops of the Seventh Army shortly after landing in Sicily searching Italian prisoners blasted out of a gun position.

II

By D-plus-10, half of Sicily was in Allied hands, and the Seventh Army began a new offensive designed to take it through to the north coast, cutting the island in two. On the morning of July 22nd, the 45th Division struck for the northern shore about 30 miles east of Palermo, while the 3rd Division and elements of the 2nd Armoured made a frontal advance on the city.

At 0530 that morning, a lone American jeep moved at a steady 30mph along the winding mountain roads towards San Stefano, on the north coast between Palermo and Termini Imerese. The vehicle was commanded by a young Lieutenant named Samuel Riley, whose regiment was spearheading the advance of the 3rd Division. Riley's job was to set up an observation post on a hill near San Stefano, an objective due to have been taken by a US infantry battalion by the time they arrived. With Riley in the jeep were Sgt Pete Tickler, Pfc Theodore Moody, Pte Hentry Lorah, Pfc Addison McCullough, and T/S Louis Johns, the driver.

The road was good, although two bridges had been blown along the way. The first obstacle they negotiated by riding the lines across a railroad span, the second by fording a shallow creek. By 0800 the sun was well up, and the summit of Mount Etna, 40 miles away on the horizon, was clearly visible. A few minutes later the Americans reached the little town of Bivona, where the population turned out to welcome them in force. Up a narrow side street they found two more jeeps from divisional reconnaissance. Their commanders told Riley that this was as far as they had penetrated. They were on the point of turning back to the first blown bridge to ferry across the rest of the reconnaissance troop and would leave Riley to carry on alone.

On a morning like this, it was hard to believe there was a war on. As the jeep purred on its way out of Bivona, the crew chatted casually of home. Suddenly, less than a mile ahead, they spotted a motor cycle. Through his binoculars, Riley saw it was Italian and mounted by two soldiers. A few seconds later it disappeared round a bend; the riders had apparently not seen the jeep.

Entering Palermo, troops of the American
Seventh Army had nearly completed two
weeks campaign in Sicily. The city fell
without resistance on 22nd July, 1943.

17

Above: In Palermo the Americans were greeted by cheering crowds.

Left: Major John L. Leidenheimer of Signals Supply, Seventh Army, took over this building formerly used by the Italians as a gigantic signals and QM Headquarters shortly after the Americans had received the surrender of Palermo.

Nevertheless, all at once the war seemed dangerously close; although the countryside remained idyllic in the morning sunlight, there was plenty of shelter for enemy snipers. Riley ordered Johns to slow down to 15mph. Stopping at every curve in the road, they went forward on foot to see what was on the other side before proceeding in the jeep.

As they rounded one curve about 3 miles short of San Stefano, an Italian soldier almost fell into their arms. He was young, dejected and terrified, but since none of the Americans could speak Italian they were unable to interrogate him. Instead, they bundled him into the jeep and took him along with them.

By this time Riley was convinced that things up ahead were not as they should be, and the sound of distant rifle-fire confirmed his anxiety. He accordingly decided to park the jeep and continue on foot up a ridge overlooking San Stefano. From this vantage point, he swept the area with his binoculars. The noise of rifle-fire increased until it reached the proportions of a minor battle. Riley assumed that the Division's 3rd Battalion had run into trouble, and decided to set up his OP on this ridge. It was only about 0930 and still pleasantly cool. The firing had stopped, so while they were waiting for something to happen the men opened a couple of cans of C-rations and sat down under a tree to have breakfast.

The ridge was about 2 miles west of San Stefano and gave them a good view of the road in and out of the town, as well as of a small railway station only 700 yards away. Everything remained quiet until halfway through the meal, when Johns suddenly spotted movement near the station. They all stopped eating; Riley focused his glasses in the direction of Johns's pointing finger and picked out an Italian soldier refreshing camouflage over a gun position. Scanning the area on either side of the railway station, Riley located several other gun positions along the road, defending the approach to the town. They were trained directly on the far side of the curve concealing Riley's jeep; another few yards and they would have met a storm of shells.

By the time Riley's party had pinpointed all the enemy positions, the two divisional recce jeeps had arrived on the scene, stopping when they saw Riley's parked vehicle. The parties were accompanied by the Colonel commanding the regiment, who joined Riley on the ridge. After assessing the situation, he ordered up all the armament available from the recce units in the area. This included one 75mm gun, two 37mm, two ·50 machine-guns and four ·30 light-machine-guns. As soon as they were all in position on the ridge, the Colonel ordered them to open fire on the enemy gun emplacements.

The 3rd Battalion, meanwhile, had been stopped. After a forced march of 52 miles in thirty-six hours to San Stefano, they encountered the small-arms fire which Riley and his men had heard and fought their way through to a hill south-east of the town. The rest of the Regiment was still some 20 miles back along the road, advancing mostly on foot but with one company motorised.

Back on the ridge, Lt Riley volunteered to take three men and attack the enemy road-block, to form a better assessment of its strength. To accompany him he chose Sgt Tickler and Ptes Moody and McCullough. Johns was to drive the jeep up to the bend in the road to stir up some sort of diversion and give cover with the machine-gun. The radio was removed from the jeep and Lorah stayed with it, to maintain contact with the Regiment. He also kept an eye on the Italian prisoner, but the latter seemed to be in no hurry to escape.

Riley and the others picked their way down the ridge from cover to cover; a creek bed and plum orchard offered fair concealment, although the creek was enfiladed by an enemy machine-gun across the road. Despite the danger, the Americans paused for a few seconds to fill their canteens at a spring in the orchard and snatch a few plums.

Meanwhile, in the jeep, Johns was having a hot time. To cover Riley and the others, he had to expose himself to heavy small-arms fire, but despite everything neither he nor the jeep was hit. He was unable to see his colleagues after they left the ridge, and concentrated on making the Italians keep their heads down.

The others, after leaving the orchard, moved cautiously up the creek bed to find out the source of the flanking fire; the machine-gun which had been the biggest source of trouble had been knocked out by this time, but some fire still came down the creek. Anticipating a fight, they were halfway to the road when they saw a white flag waving from the top of the opposite ridge. When the Americans climbed up to investigate, thirty Italians emerged from cover with their hands high. Riley turned them over to Tickler and Moody, who marched them back up the ridge.

There was no fire now from Riley's side of the road and only spasmodic bursts from the other side. Riley and McCullough made sure that there was no one left on their side before crossing the road back to the railway station. On the way back they collected twenty-two more prisoners, who surrendered without a murmur.

Meanwhile, the Colonel had managed to acquire two 105mm howitzers, which opened fire on the town. This barrage, together with the elimination of the road-block, relieved pressure on the 3rd Battalion on the other side of San Stefano. The Italians withdrew into the town and were soon observed to be evacuating it. The 3rd Battalion split into two sections and artillery fire switched to the road leading out of the town, with the result that only five enemy trucks escaped. After that, opposition in San Stefano quickly melted away and the town surrendered. Several hundred prisoners were taken, together with much material. For his part in the action, Lt Sam Riley was awarded the DSC.

The stage was now set for a rapid drive on Palermo. The 2nd Armoured Division moved up to the departure line, its left and rear covered by Task Force X, which had secured the ground between Marsala and Salemi. The 2nd Armoured pushed on from Castelvetrano through Camporeale, San Giuseppe and Monreale to the high ground 5 miles below Palermo itself. Meanwhile, the 3rd Division, deployed along high ground south-east of the city, and the 157th Infantry broke through to the main north coast road. Advancing from San Caterina, the 180th RCT also reached the outskirts of Palermo, where it linked up with the 3rd Division. A co-ordinated attack on the town was planned, but there was no resistance and Palermo surrendered at 2000 hours on July 22nd.

The capture of Palermo meant that the second phase of the Seventh Army's task in Sicily was virtually over; it now remained only for the Americans to mop-up isolated enemy pockets in the west of the island before devoting all their strength to the third and final phase: pushing the enemy back through the Messina Peninsula.

The Americans wasted no time. Twenty-four hours after the fall of Palermo, the final clean-up of western Sicily was well under way. Over 9,500 prisoners were caught in the trap, including the commanding general of all Italian coastal divisions in the west. Consolidation in the large part of Sicily now under Seventh Army control called for the immediate repairing of roads, railways and public services. A major task was to clear Palermo harbour, where sunken vessels, demolished quays and mines made the port unusable by all but small craft.

By the end of July 23rd, an enemy railway was serving the Seventh Army's advance, operating from Licata up to Campobello. A week later, the Americans found sixteen steam locomotives and 100 freight cars in the Caltanissetta marshalling yards. The work of repairing rail traffic and ports continued. A week after the town surrendered, the first coasters were unloading at Palermo, and the Americans also brought into service a quantity of rolling stock on the standard guage railway between Palermo and Messina.

The Seventh Army's advance on Messina began with a swing eastwards by II Corps, with the 18th RCT of the 1st Division reaching Gangi and forging 5 miles ahead towards Nicosia. Cefalu was taken by the 45th Division, and on July 24th the Seventh Army rounded up an incredible total of 11,540 prisoners, most of them demoralised Italians. In the area north of Alimena-Leonforte, the Americans identified all three battalions of the 3rd Panzer Grenadier Regiment, an indication that the rest of the campaign would have to be fought against predominantly German formations.

The German hold on Sicily, however, was reduced daily, and to hasten the enemy's withdrawal the Americans allocated all their available artillery to II Corps. Moreover, they gave the infantry extra fire support with newly-arrived 4·2in chemical mortars, which proved highly effective in mountainous terrain.

Suddenly, on July 26th, II Corps began to encounter stiffer resistance, indicating that the enemy's period of rapid retreat was at an end. Air reconnaissance reported an increase in the flow of enemy reinforcements across the Straits of Messina, and the Germans were also digging in west of Sperlinga. Nevertheless, the Allies continued to gain ground. On July 30th came the news that in the far west the islands of Favignana, Marettimo and Levanzo, off Trapini, had surrendered to the 82nd Airborne Division, and a sudden drop in the number of prisoners taken daily indicated that the round-up of Italians in the west was almost complete.

The 1st Division, meanwhile, had pushed on to within 5 miles of Troina, which was to be the scene of some of the bitterest fighting of the campaign. The battle for the town began on August 1st with a dusk skirmish, when 200 Germans attacked American positions on nearby high ground. They were successfully repulsed, and at 0330 on August 3rd the 1st Division jumped off on schedule to launch the attack on Troina. During the day, after a stiff fight, the 16th and 18th US Infantry took high ground west and north of the town.

At 1645 on the 4th, the softening up of Troina's main defences began with a sharp bombardment by eight and a half artillery battalions and seventy-two A-36 fighter-bombers, each of which carried a 500lb bomb. Fifty minutes later, the US infantry began their advance, but the town's battered defenders stuck doggedly to their positions and prevented any general breakthrough. As this battle raged, the US 3rd Division moved slowly eastwards along the coast near Fiume Furiano, assisted by Navy Task Force 88, which hammered enemy positions on Cape Orlando and San Agata. The 7th RCT, with attached Corps artillery, was moved by sea to the area behind the 15th RCT in readiness for an assault on the San Fratello Ridge.

It was now clear that the Germans were fighting desperately to gain time to evacuate their forces to the Italian mainland; all along the front, they yielded ground only at the cost of severe casualties. On August 5th, in the wake of a furious air bombardment, the 16th RCT of the 1st Division finally broke through into Troina, while the 60th RCT of the 9th Division fought its way up the high ground 7 miles north of the town. Further

Above: A smokescreen blots out half of Palermo—a demonstration given by Chemical Smoke Generator Companies shortly after the city had fallen.

Below: Palermo Harbour was opened for supply ships a week after the town was captured. Clearance was a major task—the retreating enemy had sunk block-ships, demolished quays and strewn the whole area with mines.

The American Seventh Army's Military Police found the field telephone essential for controlling traffic in the narrow winding roads of Sicily. Here, at Trabia, in the north of the island, a one-way system was set up not long after the last of the enemy troops had withdrawn across the Straits of Messina to the Italian mainland.

north, the 3rd Division got a foothold on the east bank of the Furiano River during August 7th, and by dark held the high ground north of San Fratello. For thirteen and a half hours afterwards, as waves of fighter-bombers attacked enemy positions on Mount Fratello, the Americans maintained a 1,000 yard long smokescreen to conceal the movements of the 7th Infantry as they prepared for the assault on San Fratello Ridge. While these preparations were under way, a force comprising the 2nd Battalion, 30th Infantry, a tank platoon of the 753rd Tank Battalion, and two batteries of the 58th Armoured Field Artillery Battalion carried out a seaborne landing at 0400 on Augst 8th. They beached at a point 2 miles east of Torrenova, south-west of Cape Orlando, and occupied high ground south of the coastal highway. This thrust in the enemy's back, combined with the attack of the 7th Infantry, broke German resistance on Mount Fratello; shortly afterwards, the town fell to the 15th and 30th Infantry. At 1600 the 7th Infantry advanced under another smokescreen to capture San Agata and make contact with the seaborne force. All enemy resistance quickly ceased around Mount Fratello, and the heights were scaled early that same day.

Mines, demolitions and road-blocks delayed the general American advance during the next forty-eight hours, but they failed to stop it. On August 11th, the enemy attempted to reform and organise a defence along the Cape Orlando-Naso line, but this was frustrated by the 3rd Division and another amphibious assault. Protected by strong air cover and supported by the guns of Naval Task Force 88, the 2nd Battalion, 30th Infantry, landed with artillery and tanks 2 miles east of the cape and captured a position astride the highway and railroad 2 miles west of Brolo. The enemy launched a furious counter-attack against the seaborne force, but the latter managed to hold its ground. Meanwhile, the 7th RCT crossed the Zappulla River and the 15th RCT entered Naso.

By August 12th, the enemy evacuation across the Straits of Messina was under way on a large scale. Air reconnaissance photographs, taken over the Straits on August 11th, showed thirty three vessels plying between Sicily and the mainland, including ten Siebel ferries.

As the Americans, British and Canadians all converged towards the north-east tip of the island, the impetus of the Allied offensive increased and the enemy defences became shallower. At Randazzo, for example, the enemy defence consisted of minefields with only sporadic artillery fire; this opposition was soon overcome by the 9th Division, which occupied the town on August 13th. In the 3rd Division's sector, the 30th RCT advanced almost as far as Patti, while the 15th RCT and the 3rd Ranger Battalion mopped up pockets of Germans to the south-west. The advance along the coast past Cape Calava, 4 miles north-west of Patti, was impeded by a large crater blown in the road at the eastern end of the Calava tunnel, where a way had been carved from the solid rock of a mountainside, and LCT's were used to ferry the artillery and infantry past it.

On the night of August 15th/16th, the third and last amphibious landing took place on the north coast. The 157th Infantry of the 45th Division were due to land in the vicinity of Falcone, but the American troops had thrust overland so fast that the landing zone was switched to the beaches north-west of Barcelona. The actual landing went ahead without incident, the 157th going ashore at 0230.

By August 16th, it was clear that the end in Sicily was very close. On this day, the first Allied shells fell on the Italian mainland when guns of the 36th Field Artillery fired 100 rounds of 155mm high explosive across the Straits, aiming at enemy batteries in the vicinity of Villa San Giovanni. The 7th Infantry struck out across country from Spadaforma towards its objective on a ridge 4 miles west of Messina, and during the evening the Americans pushed strong patrols into the town itself. There was no resistance. That same night the last German forces evacuated the island, leaving a considerable amount of material behind.

The 7th Infantry led the 3rd Division into Messina at daybreak on the 17th, while the 30th Infantry advanced along the northern coastal road to Cape de Faro, mopping up isolated groups of German stragglers—many of them in civilian clothes. At 1000 a small group of British tanks joined the 3rd Division in Messina, and fifteen minutes later General Patton himself also arrived.

The fall of Messina marked the fall of Sicily. Thirty-eight days after the Allies had first set foot on the island, the campaign was over. The first United States field army to fight as a unit in World War II had successfully accomplished its mission; the long, hard months of training had paid dividends.

Nevertheless, there was no escaping the fact that the enemy had avoided a crushing defeat. The Germans and Italians had lost some 12,000 killed and wounded and close on 100,000 prisoners, as well as 267 aircraft, 293 guns and 188 tanks; but the Germans had succeeded in evacuating 40,000 troops, 9,600 vehicles, 94 guns, 47 tanks, 1,000 tons of ammunition, 970 tons of fuel and 15,700 tons of other material. The Italians, for their part, evacuated between 70,000 and 75,000 men.

The Allied losses included 11,500 British and 7,500 Americans killed, wounded or missing. Such was the price of the campaign that swung the balance of the war in Europe in favour of the Allies. The close of the campaign, however, left the Allies with few grounds for over-optimism.

The British and Americans—particularly the latter, who were relatively new to combat—had been surprised by the strength of enemy resistance. The ability of the Germans and Italians to fight a gigantic delaying action for so long with one-third as many combat troops as the Allies had been no mean military achievement, particularly in view of the deteriorating Italo-German Alliance.

The battle in Sicily was an indication that the struggle ahead would be long and hard. It would be many months yet before the Seventh Army reached the end of the arduous road that was to lead it to the heart of the Third Reich.

Corned beef and tomato juice for the Seventh Army being unloaded at Highway Division's Dump 1, Palermo, Sicily.

III

On December 19th, 1943, Allied Force Headquarters sent a telegram to Seventh Army Headquarters in Palermo. It read: "An estimate is required as a matter of urgency as to the accommodations which you would require for your planning staffs should you be asked to undertake the planning of an operation of a similar size to Husky* . . ."

Since the end of the Sicilian campaign, the Seventh Army had been cut from a tactical force of six divisions to a headquarters, with a few remaining service units manned by skeleton staffs. The invasion of Italy had begun on August 17th, and by the end of 1943 speculation had reached fever pitch as to the date of an Allied landing in northern Europe. Now, after months of relative inactivity, the Seventh Army knew that it was to take part in an operation comparable to the Sicilian landings, and in the last week of December preparations were made to organise a planning staff for it at a point just outside Algiers.

On December 29th, Allied Force HQ revealed some details of the proposed operation, which was to be known under the codename of 'Anvil' to senior Seventh Army officers. It involved a series of landings on the south coast of France, to be launched in conjunction with Operation 'Overlord'—the assault on north-west Europe—and was designed to create a Mediterranean bridgehead. Two early objectives of the invasion were Lyons and Vichy, the seat of the French Government, and the operation was to be undertaken by American and Free French forces.

On January 1st, 1944, Lieutenant-General Mark W. Clark replaced General Patton as commander of the Seventh Army, and under his direction planning for 'Anvil' went ahead rapidly. In mid-January, while the planners were selecting target beaches in southern France, the Allied landings were launched at Anzio in Italy—a bold move which, had it progressed successfully, would have meant the release of large Allied forces for future operations in the Mediterranean. It was soon apparent, however, that the Allies at Anzio were in serious trouble, and that consequently there was little likelihood of substantial forces from that quarter becoming available in time for 'Anvil'. It was, at this stage, thought improbable that more than two divisions—with two more in reserve—could be allocated.

On February 10th, 1944, D-Day for Operation 'Overlord' was postponed by about three weeks. The shipping requirements for this operation were also proving so enormous that the Mediterranean Theatre had to return to Britain all landing craft not vitally needed. As February passed and the Italian campaign began to get bogged down in the face of stiff enemy resistance, it was realised that General Clark could not cope with the planning of 'Anvil' as well as the growing strain of the Fifth Army's war in Italy, so on March 2nd he was succeeded in command of the Seventh Army by Lieutenant-General Alexander M. Patch.

Time was now getting drastically short, and as the target date for the launching of 'Anvil' was still early June, Patch requested the immediate designation of the American divisions which were to take part in the invasion. Shortly afterwards, because of projected offensives in Italy and the wholesale transfer of landing craft to 'Overlord', it was decided that 'Anvil' could not possibly be launched before late July.

On April 29th, the outline plans for 'Anvil' were presented to the Supreme Allied Commander, Mediterranean Theatre. They called for a parachute force of at least three battalions to support an initial two-division assault, while Commandos and Rangers were to be assigned special missions to neutralise offshore islands, block roads and protect the flanks of the main assault. The proposed target area was east of Toulon, between Cape Cavalaire and the Bay of Agay. The Air Force was to provide close tactical support throughout, and was also to initiate a programme of pre-invasion bombing from Spain to the Italian border. The Navy would co-operate in reducing enemy coastal defences.

On May 13th, three alternative plans were drawn up, each dictated by an assumption of the enemy's reaction to the landings. Plan A envisaged a partial German withdrawal, Plan B a complete evacuation of southern France, and Plan C total surrender and the cessation of all organised resistance. The likeliest of the three, Plan A, allowed for a two-divisional assault in the area east of Toulon, with a target date early in August. The capture of Toulon and Marseilles was its main objective, followed by an exploitation northward towards Lyons and Vichy. The assumption was that the enemy would offer resistance on the beaches, but would withdraw the greater part of his forces from the coastal area, fighting heavy delaying actions in the lower Rhône Valley

The Combined Chiefs of Staff clearly took the view that France would be the decisive theatre of operations during 1944, and the Supreme Commander, General Eisenhower, recommended that 'Anvil' should be launched not later than August 30th, preferably by August 15th. The final go-ahead reached Seventh Army HQ on June 23rd, and marked the beginning of the most intense phase of planning and training.

The Mediterranean coast of France consists of three main mountain masses separated by two corridors: the Pyrenees along the Spanish border, the Massif Central in the middle, and the French Alps in the east towards the Italian-Swiss border. The latter two masses are separated by the Valley of the Rhône River, which flows through a series of defiles and broad basins. Below Avignon, the Rhône Valley widens into an extensive delta which becomes a long stretch of marshy coast stretching from the base of the Pyrenees to Marseilles. The general bogginess of this area ruled it out for a landing; so 'Anvil' had to aim farther east, where the coast was rugged and irregular with mountains reaching down to the sea, leaving only narrow sandy beaches and small plains. Passage into the interior was possible through only a few narrow river valleys such as the Argens, which formed the best approach to the Rhône Valley from the south. It was this stretch of coast, from the Bay of Cavalaire to the Rade d'Agay, that was chosen as the target for Operation 'Anvil'.

To defend the south coast of France, the Nineteenth German Army had at its disposal nine divisions, spread thinly along the Mediterranean and at various strategic points in the interior. German naval power in the Mediterranean at this stage of the war was almost non-existent, amounting only to ten U-boats and a handful of small surface vessels. First-line aircraft numbered about 1,500, including 200 in the area of the projected Allied landing. The Germans were aware of the possibility of an invasion on the French Mediterranean coast, but they had no way of knowing when and where it would fall. Their defensive policy, therefore, consisted mainly of laying mines in strips along the coast, off-shore defences being largely restricted to areas of the big ports. For coastal defence, they relied on artillery of every description: railway guns, field pieces, old French and Italian equipment, and naval guns transferred from French warships scuttled in Toulon harbour. Local defences along the coast did not run very deep; they were based on a system of strong-points comprising concrete pillboxes, barbed-wire and minefields, in most cases expertly camouflaged. The Allies could also expect to encounter road-blocks and antitank obstacles, as well as minefields in road beds from the beaches to the main lateral highway.

The main Allied assault zone extended some 45 miles along the Riviera coast and included sixteen target beaches. These were numbered in series from west to east and were grouped into three principal assault areas known as Alpha, Delta and Camel. On August 1st, 1944, the codename of the operation was changed from 'Anvil' to 'Dragoon'. The final outline plans for the assault were as follows:

Army Ground and Airborne Plan
General mission: to establish a beachhead east of Toulon as a base for the assault, to capture Toulon and then Marseilles and exploit towards Lyons and Vichy. To carry out this task, the following forces were available.

KODAK FORCE, consisting of VI Corps Headquarters and its assigned units: the 3rd, 45th and 36th Infantry Divisions, plus one French Armoured Combat Command and supporting troops. Kodak's mission was to land three reinforced infantry divisions at H-Hour on the beaches between Cape Cavalaire and Agay. A rapid advance was to be made inland to contact the Airborne Task Force. As soon as the beaches were cleared, the French Armoured Combat Command would land. The beachhead was to be extended to the Blue Line, the D-plus-2 objective, and airfield sites secured in the Argens Valley between Fréjus and Le Muy. Further advances to the west and north-west would protect the right flank of the Army; after the French II Corps was established ashore, contact was to be maintained. Kodak would be prepared to release the French Armoured Combat Command, the French Groupe de Commandos and all airborne forces to Army control on demand.

The French commitment, known as GARBO FORCE, consisted of a detachment of HQ French Army B, the French II Corps with the 1st French Motorised, 3rd Algerian, and 9th Colonial Infantry Divisions plus the 1st French Armoured Division— less one Combat Command—and supporting troops. Landing in the St Tropez-Cavalaire area on D-plus-1, the French were to pass through the left of the US VI Corps and capture Toulon. By D plus 9, the French 9th Colonial Division was to be landed in the Le Lavandou-Hyères area, the remainder of the 1st French Armoured Division was to be ashore by D-plus-25. After the capture of Toulon, the attack was to be continued in the direction of Marseilles and to the north-west, the French maintaining contact on the right with the US VI Corps.

RUGBY FORCE was the name allocated to the Seventh Army Provisional Airborne Division, composed of the 2nd British Independent Parachute Brigade, one Parachute RCT, two Parachute Battalions, one Infantry Glider Battalion and supporting troops. This force was to land on the high ground north and east of Le Muy and on the high ground north of

Grimaud. The primary mission was to prevent the movement of enemy forces into the assault area from the west and north-west. Le Muy was to be cleared of enemy forces before dark on D-Day and the area secured for subsequent glider landings; Rugby Force's task was to assault enemy positions from the rear and assist the advance of the seaborne forces by neutralising as many enemy installations as possible. Bridges in the Airborne Division area were to be prepared for demolition, but none were to be blown except on the orders of the Task Force Commander. As soon as contact with the seaborne force was established, Rugby Force was to revert to US VI Corps control.

SITKA FORCE, comprising the 1st Special Service Force, was to land under cover of darkness prior to H-Hour and neutralise all enemy defences on the Islands of Port Cros and Levant. It would subsequently be prepared to withdraw to the mainland and reorganise under the name of SATAN FORCE for the capture of the Island of Porquerolles.

ROMEO FORCE, the French Groupe de Commandos, was to land under cover of darkness before H-Hour and destroy enemy defences on Cap Nègre. The coastal highway in the vicinity of the Cape was to be blocked and the high ground 2 miles to the north seized. Romeo Force would protect the left flank of the assault and would eventually come under control of VI Corps.

The last assault unit, ROSIE FORCE, consisted of the French Naval Assault Group, a demolition party which was to land in the vicinity of the Pointe de Trayas on the night before D-Day. Its mission was to carry out demolition work on the Cannes-St Raphaël and Cannes-Fréjus highways, and then fall back on the Army's right flank.

Naval Plan
The mission of the Eighth Fleet was to establish the Seventh Army firmly ashore and to support its advance westward for the capture of Toulon and Marseilles. The Fleet was responsible for the Army build-up on the beach and its maintenance, until the capture of the ports simplified the logistics task. To carry out its mission the Navy was subdivided into six forces, each with a specific task.

The CONTROL FORCE was to provide naval beach control and establish and operate naval fuel facilities on shore in the assault area. Navigational markers and air beacon markers were to be established, and diversionary operations carried out. The Control Force would protect the assault convoys from hostile surface or submarine units, and would provide convoy control and escort for shipping outside the assault area.

ALPHA ATTACK FORCE was to establish the 3rd US Infantry Division on selected beaches in the Pampelonne-Cavalaire area, beginning at H-Hour on D-Day. On D-plus-1, it would begin landing advance units of French Army B. It was to position five pontoon causeways on Beach 261 and five on Beach 259, and at the earliest opportunity unload special Air Force equipment on the Island of Port Cros. Its naval guns would eliminate enemy batteries threatening transports, landing craft or the beaches themselves.

The task of DELTA ATTACK FORCE was to establish the 45th Infantry Division on selected beaches in the St Tropez-Bougnon area at H-Hour; it was also to deliver five pontoon causeways to beach 261 and exploit the port facilities of St Tropez. On D-plus-1, Delta Force was to assist Alpha Force in landing elements of French Army B.

The third Naval Attack Force, CAMEL, was to establish the US 36th Infantry Division and one Combat Command of the 1st French Armoured Division on the St Raphaël-Anthéor beaches beginning at H-Hour. As soon as the beaches were cleared, it was to prepare to land another French Combat Command. The Force was to ensure that platoon causeways were delivered to Beach 259 for unloading French armoured equipment.

A SUPPORT FORCE, meanwhile, was to establish the 1st Special Service Force (Sitka) on the Islands of Levant and Port Cros, and the French Groupe de Commandos (Romeo) in the vicinity of Cape Nègre. Its bombardment would support the military operations, and after the initial assault phases the Force would continue to support the Army's westward advance.

The sixth of the naval subdivisions, the AIRCRAFT CARRIER FORCE, was to provide fighter cover, reconnaissance and close support and was to be prepared to transfer combat units to captured airfields.

Air Plan
The Commanding General of the XII Tactical Air Command, Brigadier-General Gordon P. Saville, was designated the Air Task Force Commander and charged with all detailed air planning for Operation 'Dragoon'. From the point of view of time, air operations were broken down into four phases. Phase I covered offensive air operations before D-minus-5; Phase II covered D-minus-5 to 0350 on D-Day; Phase III, 0350 on D-Day to H-Hour at 0800; and Phase IV the period after H-Hour.

PHASE I air operations had begun as far back as April 28th, 1944, when heavy bombers attacked Toulon. Between then and August 10th, the Allied Air Forces had dropped more than 12,500 tons of bombs on southern France.

PHASE II, known as Operation 'Nutmeg'—beginning on August 10th—was to consist primarily of attacks on coastal defences and radar stations, at the same time isolating the target area by destroying highway bridges across the Rhône River. In order not to jeopardise tactical surprise, this phase was to be carried out in conjunction with feint attacks on similar targets between Via Reggio in Italy and Béziers, near the Franco-Spanish border. The intensity of the attacks along such a broad front would, it was hoped, conceal the true Allied objectives until at least 1800 on D-minus-1.

PHASE III (Operation 'Yokum') was to begin one hour after the conclusion of 'Nutmeg' and last until H-Hour. Its main task was to inflict maximum destruction on enemy coastal and beach defences, using all available forces. These included twelve heavy bomber groups, plus medium and fighter bombers. The latter were to attack coastal batteries, while the heavy bombers were to strike at the assault beaches to flatten underwater obstacles and enemy strongpoints.

PHASE IV (Operation 'Ducrot'), beginning after H-Hour, would interdict enemy communications by completing the destruction of bridges over the Rhône and Isère Rivers, as well as giving tactical close support to ground forces.

The task of airlifting the Seventh Army Airborne Division, which consisted of both parachute and gliderborne troops, was assigned to the Provisional Troop Carrier Air Division. From bases in Italy, they were to employ thirty-two squadrons of transport aircraft—415 in all, escorted by *Spitfires* and *Beaufighters*—operating from bases in Italy. The first drops were to be made just before daylight on D-Day, and the first re-supply mission was to be flown in the late afternoon.

The total troop list, revised on July 30th, stood at 155,419 men and 20,031 vehicles. The subsequent build-up would put 366,833 men and 56,051 vehicles ashore by D-plus-30, and 576,833 men and 91,341 vehicles by D-plus-65. Since no units were assigned to the Seventh Army until the middle of June, 1944—after the Normandy landings—their period of training was necessarily brief. Nevertheless, the two months before D-Day gave sufficient time for the main combat elements of each of the three American sub-task forces to undergo a refresher course in amphibious assault. The 36th and 45th Divisions received their instruction at the Invasion Training

Centre at Salerno, while the 3rd Division went to Pozzuoli.

At the end of the landing exercises, the three American assault divisions moved up to Naples for mounting; the French force was to be embarked at Taranto, Corsica and Oran. On August 9th, General Lucian K. Truscott, the VI Corps Commander, briefed his staff, and two days later General Patch conducted his final briefing at Seventh Army HQ in Naples.

On the afternoon of August 11th, the Chief of Staff and other personnel boarded the USS *Henrico* in the Bay of Naples. Here the Seventh Army set up its command while the vast amphibious force prepared for the assault. The various elements of the Seventh Army were waiting at embarkation ports in Italy, Corsica and North Africa. The 3rd Infantry Division under Major-General John W. O'Daniel, the 36th Division commanded by Major-General John E. Dahlquist, and the 45th Division under Major-General William W. Eagles were all assembled in the Naples-Salerno area; the French II Corps lay in harbours on the heel of Italy, the 1st Special Service Force was off Corsica, and near Oran in Algeria were minor elements of II Corps and Combat Command One of the 1st French Armoured Division.

The approach corridor for the assault was the stretch of water between the north-west coast of Corsica and the beaches, and the 'Dragoon' convoys were to converge on it via ten separate routes. The Western Task Force, commanded by Vice-Admiral Hewitt, consisted of 853 vessels: 505 US ships, 252 British, 19 French, 6 Greek, and 263 merchant vessels. There were 370 large landing ships, escorted by 5 battleships, 4 heavy cruisers, 18 light cruisers, 9 aircraft carriers and 85 destroyers. Deck-loaded on the transports were 1,267 small landing craft.

The Alpha, Delta and Camel attack forces set sail from their respective harbours on August 11th, 12th and 13th, the slower vessels leaving first. Units had received maps in sealed packages seventy-two hours before embarking, together with the Seventh Army identification code and its key. These were to be opened four hours after sailing and all assault troops were carefully briefed. The Americans were issued with special shoulder patches and flag brassards, which they sewed on their uniforms.

The voyage passed peacefully, the great convoys edging northward along the west coast of Italy and then negotiating the Straits of Bonifacio as planned. At about 1900 on August 14th, off the west coast of Corsica, the 'Dragoon' convoys made their rendezvous and turned towards their objectives on the French Riviera. Before the main assault on the Cogolin-St Tropez-Ste Maxime-St Raphaël coastline, plans to isolate the invasion area by commando forces on the flanks went into operation. Ships of the Support Force slipped out of Propriano, Corsica, at 1130 on August 14th, and soon after dark the sharp silhouettes of the cliffs of Levant and Port Cros appeared.

The weather was ideal, with a calm sea and a night dark enough yet with sufficient starlight for the assault forces to pick out prominent landmarks. The big transports stopped engines about 8,000 yards out, and at 2300 hours the troops embarked in ten-man rubber boats. Each LCI towed nine of these boats to within 1,000 yards of the shore, and as they paddled quietly on, scouts in kayaks and electric surf-floats went ahead to mark the landing spots with small lights. About 650 men landed on Port Cros and 1,300 on Levant at midnight. The planners had selected the southern side of the islands for the attack, where steep cliffs dropped straight into the sea, and the assault achieved complete surprise. The enemy had discounted all possibility of an attack from this direction, and the landings met no opposition. Scattered resistance broke out on Levant, but the enemy soon withdrew and by dawn the assault forces were landing supplies and evacuating their wounded. Mopping-up continued throughout D-Day, with only snipers and isolated pockets still resisting in the afternoon. At 2234, all opposition on Levant ceased. On Port Cros, an enemy garrison in an old fort on the western side of the island managed to hold out for forty-eight hours before the fight ended with the surrender of two German officers and forty-six men.

Meanwhile, shortly after midnight, the 'Romeo' force of French commandos landed on Cape Nègre. Their mission was to destroy all enemy coastal defences on the Cape, to set up a road-block on the coastal highway and to seize the high ground 2 miles to the north. Seventy men scaled the steep banks at the base of the Cape, taking the Germans by surprise. They quickly destroyed the enemy gun emplacements and set up a tank-block in a pass along the road. The other detachment had as its objective a series of pillboxes believed to be east of the Cape. One section, however, landed too close to the Cape and was greeted by small-arms fire and grenades. The section was pinned down and several men killed and wounded, including Sgt Noel Texier, its commander. This group of French commandos attracted the attention of most of the enemy defences, with the result that when the main body of Romeo Force landed at 0100 they were almost unopposed. By morning, the Commandos had cleared the beaches and joined up with the others who were holding the tank-block; they then advanced inland to clear the towns of Le Rayol and La Mole, beating off several enemy counter-attacks.

During the night, the Rosie Force of sixty-seven French Marines was landed from four torpedo-boats in seven rubber craft on the beach south of Théoule-sur-Mer. Rosie's objectives were the roads from Cannes to St

Raphaël and Fréjus, aiming at cutting enemy communications between Cannes and the right flank of the main assault. In the darkness, however, the Marines ran into barbed-wire, then anti-personnel mines. The explosions alerted the enemy. The Germans immediately opened up a deadly fire over the flat beach. The Marines abandoned their demolition equipment and tried to pull back, but they were hopelessly trapped, and many were killed and wounded. The survivors eventually made contact with the Americans the next afternoon, and their injured were evacuated by the 56th Medical Battalion.

The main pre-invasion operation was the airborne assault. To isolate the entire landing area, the coastal highway had to be cut at each end of the beachhead and enemy movements blocked from the rear. The 1st Airborne Task Force, known as Rugby, had the mission of landing from 0430 near Le Muy and Le Luc to set up road-blocks and so help reduce the enemy defences in the beach area itself.

The Airborne Task Force had been created specifically for this assault. Activated on July 15th, under the command of General Robert T Frederick, it comprised the 2nd Independent Parachute Brigade (British), the 517th Parachute Infantry Regiment, the 509th Parachute Infantry Battalion, the 1st Battalion of the 551st Parachute Infantry Regiment, the 460th Parachute Field Artillery Battalion, the 463rd Parachute Field Artillery Battalion, the 550th Glider Infantry Battalion and the 602nd Glider Pack Howitzer Battalion. There were also gliderborne supporting troops such as two chemical mortar companies and an antitank company. The total strength was 9,732 men, to be transported in 535 transport aircraft and 465 gliders.

Aerial routes marked by beacon ships were set up east of the assault corridor from Corsica. The three drop zones were designated O, A and C, two of them, O and A, consisted of flat cultivated fields or gently undulating ground suitable for both paratroop and glider operations, but C was a less desirable broken, rocky area.

On D-Day, the drop zones were shrouded in fog, and in the murk many of the parachute elements fell a long way from their objective. The first to jump was the 509th Battalion Combat Team at 0430, followed by the 517th Regimental Combat Team five minutes later. Part of Lieutenant-Colonel William P. Yarborough's 509th Battalion came down on the banks of the Nartuby River near La Motte, while Colonel William J. Boyle and forty men of the 517th, cut off from the rest of their 1st Battalion, were met by heavy machine-gun fire as they landed in hamlets and vineyards near Les Arcs. Boyle and his men returned the fire and deployed over the area, precipitating the first pitched battle of the campaign.

At 0510, detachments of the British 2nd Independent Parachute Brigade landed more or less on target in the hills of Le Rouet, east of Le Mitan, and the 2nd Battalion of the 517th Regiment under Colonel Richard J. Seitz pushed rapidly towards Les Arcs to relieve Boyle's force. Although this part of the drop was fairly successful, however, it took some of the airborne units twenty-four hours—and in some cases several days—to reach their assembly areas. Some, including parts of the 509th Parachute Battalion and the 463rd Parachute Artillery Battalion, never made it at all. Nevertheless, most units of the First Airborne Task Force were able to go into action as soon as they landed and carry out their basic tasks. That the 463rd Battalion was dropped in the wrong place, in fact, turned out to be unexpectedly useful. The Battalion was scheduled to land in Zone C, but in the foggy conditions one serial of twenty-nine aircraft got lost and dropped their loads a long way off target. Two full batteries and sections of two more dropped in the 3rd Infantry Division's area about 3 miles south of St Tropez, close to formidable enemy coastal installations and right in the target area of Allied bombers and warships. The paratroops managed to weather the bombardment by their own ships and aircraft, and although shaken up they suffered no casualties. Somehow they managed to assemble in the strange surroundings and thick dawn fog, put five of their own guns into action, and capture intact an enemy antiaircraft battery, two coastal batteries and a garrison of 240 German soldiers. Part of one American battery, along with elements of the 509th Parachute Infantry Battalion, entered St Tropez and occupied the town. When the forward troops of the 15th Infantry Regiment, 3rd Division, eventually reached St Tropez in the wake of the seaborne landings, they found the paratroops attacking the last German defenders in a local strongpoint known as the Citadel.

Back at Le Muy, the British 2nd Independent Parachute Brigade blocked the highway there, but were unable to take the town. This task was subsequently assigned to the 550th Glider Infantry Battalion, which landed later and in greater strength. By the end of D-Day-plus-1, the First Airborne Task Force had destroyed all enemy resistance in its various zones and had taken 493 prisoners. During the entire airborne operation, no gliders or aircraft were lost through enemy action, although at least 148 gliders were wrecked or damaged in landing accidents. During the airborne assault, 987 sorties were flown, 407 gliders towed, 221 jeeps and 213 artillery pieces carried, in addition to ammunition and supplies.

The immediate mission of the airborne assault had gone well, despite some initial confusion. Prior to H-Hour, the rear of the invasion beaches had been successfully secured. It was now up to the Seventh Army's seaborne assault.

IV

The whole coastline seemed to be aflame. For 45 miles along the coast of southern France, great geysers of smoke and earth rose skywards, piercing the morning fog that rolled down to the sea. Massive concussions intermingled to form a continuous, deafening roll of sound reaching out across the Mediterranean to the ships of the invasion fleet. The air attack had opened at 0550, with wave after wave of Allied bombers—glowing like red drops of blood as the rising sun sought them out high above the mist and the shadows—hammering the beaches from Cavalaire to Anthéor. Not one German flak battery responded; the defenders, dazed by the size and fury of the holocaust, crouched in their bunkers and trembled as giant shock-waves ripped through the earth.

The huge air onslaught ended at 0730, to be succeeded by a thundering barrage from the Allied warships offshore. From one end of the invasion front to the other, 400 guns unleashed a torrent of steel on the beaches, the coastal highways and the hills beyond. Then the naval bombardment also ceased, and an eerie silence fell over the shore.

0750, and a wave of small craft raced in towards the smouldering beaches. They were drones, laden with explosives and controlled by radio from special landing craft. Their task was to blow gaps in the ranks of underwater obstacles and clear lanes right up to the beaches before the infantry went in. All but three of the drones detonated properly; one got out of control and headed back towards the fleet, exploding soon afterwards and damaging a naval vessel.

A mile offshore, positioned just behind the landing craft, the crews of over forty more vessels waited to go into action. These were rocket ships, each armed with 700 rocket-launching tubes, and at exactly 0755 they sent 30,000 flaming missiles screaming towards the beaches. One observer compared their effect to "a mammoth whip lashing the coastline". In the wake of this bombardment, at 0758, hundreds of LCIs and LCTs shot out

Above: 'The whole coastline seemed to be aflame . . . . along the coast of southern France . . . . at 0758 hundreds of LCIs and LCTs shot out through the mist towards the shore'. Men of the 3rd Division, Seventh Army, come ashore at Alpha Red Beach in the Bay of Cavalaire, France, on D-Day of Operation 'Dragoon', 15th August, 1944.

Below: Anti-aircraft half-tracks of the 3rd Division, Seventh Army, come ashore.

through the mist towards the shore. They carried the troops of the 45th Division in the centre, the 3rd on the left and the 36th on the right.

On the left flank, the 3rd Division was to assault two beaches on the St Tropez Peninsula, and for this purpose was split into two forces. Alpha Red was to hit Beach 259 in the Bay of Cavalaire, while Alpha Yellow was to go in on Beach 261 in the Bay of Pampelonne. After the peninsula had been cleared, the 3rd Division was to go to the assistance of the 45th at Beach 262, and then advance west and south-west along the coast to contact Romeo Force, the French Groupe de Commandos.

At 0800, seconds after the rocket barrage lifted, the 7th Infantry Combat Team stormed ashore on Beach 259 and the 15th Infantry on Beach 261. With each team went a smoke detail from the 3rd Chemical Battalion, four amphibious tanks from the 756th Tank Battalion, four tank destroyers of the 601st Tank Destroyer Battalion, Naval Shore Fire Control parties, and a section of the 36th Combat Engineers. Among the first to land were 154 picked troops under Colonel Wiley H. O'Mahundro, all of them sharpshooters and veterans of the Anzio and Sicily landings. Behind them came a rifle company of the 7th Infantry, but this force ran into trouble before it actually reached the shoreline. The assault craft encountered rows of concrete tetrahedrons studded with Teller mines, and several of the boats were destroyed with some sixty casualties. The demolition crews then moved in to clear the way for following craft, and within minutes waves of infantry were swarming like ants up the beaches. There was still no sign of enemy resistance. Meanwhile, amphibious tanks were being launched from LCTs lying 2,000 yards offshore. Three of the four assigned to Alpha Red Beach got ashore safely, but the fourth received a direct hit from a naval rocket falling short and the tank commander was killed. The tank limped on, only to be sunk by a mine close to the beach.

At 0825, as the engineers of the 36th Division were clearing obstructions along the waterline, the Germans suddenly emerged from their bomb shelters and opened fire with small-arms, mortars and 88mm guns. But it was too late for them to organise any real defence; by this time the amphibious tanks, tank destroyers and howitzers were all in position, and they returned the fire vigorously. The 7th continued to advance across the peninsula against only light opposition, taking a few dazed prisoners on the way.

As the rest of the regiment moved over the beach, battle patrols fanned out on the flanks to silence small-arms fire while the engineers went on with their task of clearing lanes through the minefields and wire. The work went ahead rapidly, and at 0850 a violet smoke signal informed the invasion force that the beach defences had been neutralised and that the

Above: 3rd Division troops take cover as a mine explodes near Alpha Red Beach on the St Tropez Peninsula.

Below: During the first three hours of the Seventh Army's landing in Southern France, vital unloading operations were concealed by smokescreens. Here a screen is being laid upwind just after the invasion had begun.

Division Reserve—the 30th Infantry—could land. The 30th came ashore ten minutes later and began to move forward through the right flank of the 7th.

Eight successive waves of troops went ashore on schedule at Alpha Red, enlarging the beachhead steadily. Supported by tanks and tank destroyers, the two regimental combat teams moved inland on both flanks. The 7th Infantry veered westward; its 3rd Battalion took the coastal road, clearing Cavalaire-sur-Mer, and by 1330 the Americans had reached a road-block near Cape Nègre held by the French Commandos of Romeo Force. The 2nd Battalion on the right meanwhile, passed La Croix to ascend high ground along the road running through the centre of the peninsula. When relieved by the 30th RCT at 1430, the 2nd Battalion turned south-west towards La Mole, following the 1st Battalion. The 1st had been released from reserve on the beach at noon and passed through La Mole as darkness fell on August 15th.

Over on the right flank of the 3rd Division, the 15th RCT beached on time at H-Hour on Alpha Yellow and overwhelmed all local defences within forty minutes. The 2nd Battalion, 36th Engineers, at once began clearing the shore of mines and laying pontoons for LST landings, since the gradient was too shallow for ships to approach close enough to the beach. Three out of four amphibious tanks got in safely, but the fourth was swamped by speeding landing craft as they passed it, and one of the three that did reach the shore was later disabled by a broken track.

The men advanced cautiously through sporadic small-arms fire. The 1st Battalion cleaned out an enemy strongpoint and then pushed three miles inland to take high ground, while the 2nd and 3rd Battalions made a northward arc to seize the uplands overlooking St Tropez. The 2nd actually advanced to the western edge of the town, where they wiped out another German strongpoint. Later, the French Forces of the Interior got word through that the town was virtually clear and that the population would welcome the Americans. At 1500, the 3rd Battalion reached the outskirts of St Tropez to find the American paratroops mentioned earlier and FFI assaulting the Citadel. This fell at 1830, and soon afterwards patrols of the 15th Infantry cleared all the peninsula of enemy troops.

While the 7th Infantry advanced from the beach and the 15th were clearing the peninsula, the 30th landed at H-plus-1 and passed through the 7th to take Cogolin and Grimaud. Both towns were occupied after a forced march across country, and at 2100 the 30th's patrols made contact with the 157th Infantry of the 45th Division.

Back on the beaches, the engineers continued to clear mines and demolish obstacles. Lack of gasoline soon became critical, as three-quarters of the initial supplies ferried ashore had consisted of ammunition, but in the afternoon the balance was restored as the breakthrough and advance extended the beachhead. Unloading operations during the first three hours were concealed by a heavy smokescreen.

At the end of D-Day, statistics showed a total of 264 casualties on the two Alpha beaches, 203 on Red and 61 on Yellow. The 3rd Division had taken 1,600 prisoners.

Next to the Alpha Force, the 45th Infantry Division, commanded by Major-General William W. Eagles, prepared to land in the centre of the VI Corps's assault area at H-Hour. Their mission was to clear the assault beaches and then push inland to link up with the airborne forces at Le Muy. On the west and east flanks, they were to make contact with the 3rd and 36th Infantry Divisions respectively. The three small beaches selected for the 45th's assault lay about 1 mile east of Ste Maxime, along a curving bay between Cape Sardineau and Point Alexandre. The left beach was designated Delta Red and Delta Green, while the centre and right beaches were Delta Yellow and Delta Blue. The Blue Line target for the initial expansion of the invasion ran inland 15 to 20 miles, near Le Muc and Le Muy.

The 45th Division came ashore under good amphibious conditions, with four battalions abreast. The 3rd Battalion, 157th Infantry, landed on Delta Red; the 1st Battalion, 157th Infantry, on Delta Green; the 2nd Battalion, 180th Infantry, on Delta Yellow; and the 1st Battalion, 180th Infantry, on Delta Blue. The first three waves landed on schedule, hindered only slightly by mines, underwater obstacles and light enemy resistance. The enemy beach defences had been virtually obliterated by the pre-invasion bombardment, particularly the barrage laid down by the heavy guns of two battleships: the British *Ramillies* and the French *Lorraine*.

While the 1st and 2nd Battalions of the 157th pushed inland, the 3rd Battalion attacked towards Ste Maxime. French civilians told the troops that some 500 Germans had moved out of the town at 0800, but when the advance elements reached the outskirts the enemy opened fire from a pillbox on the quay and from street barricades. This opposition was quickly dealt with by field artillery and tank destroyers. Moving into Ste Maxime from the north, I Company of the 3rd Battalion ran into heavy fire that heralded two hours of stiff house-to-house combat. Wherever possible, the Americans cleared up small pockets of resistance with hand-grenades. Two strongpoints continued to hold out after the others had surrendered; one was in the Hotel du Nord, the other in the dock zone. K Company joined I in a concerted attack on the hotel, which fell after a fierce battle. The 3rd Battalion then moved along the coast and at 2100 they contacted

Above: In the first group of prisoners captured by the Seventh Army were many Russians who claimed they had been forced to fight for the Germans. Here are some of those taken on Alpha Red Beach.

Below: Early casualties in the invasion were carried back to the beaches and shipped to the convoys offshore in LSTs.

the 3rd Division, confirming that all enemy resistance along the stretch covered by the Alpha and Delta assault areas had been eliminated.

Meanwhile, the Regimental Combat Team of Colonel Robert Dunaley's 180th Infantry landed on Delta Yellow and Delta Blue. On the latter, the 1st Battalion went ashore without opposition and proceeded to scale the sea wall. The landing of the mechanised support, however, was less successful, and the four amphibious tanks from the 191st Tank Battalion were put out of action by mines as they rolled on to the beach before lanes had been swept for them. On the adjacent Delta Yellow beach, a single tank landed while the others stayed on the waterline, firing at enemy targets until a path was cleared for them. Only one was knocked out.

The 2nd Battalion, 180th Infantry, also assaulted Delta Yellow, the supporting amphibious tanks quickly knocking out four enemy pillboxes. Here, too, one tank was immobilised by a mine. The Battalion fanned out over the deserted beach, suffering only five casualties, and advanced towards the high ground beyond.

At H-plus-1, the 3rd Battalion, 180th Infantry, followed the 1st Battalion ashore on Delta Blue Beach. A few minutes later the Americans sighted a group of enemy troops, in trucks and on bicycles, heading for a hill that dominated the beach area. The 3rd Battalion immediately opened up with machine-guns and mortars, killing a dozen Germans and driving the rest away. The Americans took the hill before nightfall.

General Eagles landed at 1100, and during the afternoon General Truscott, the VI Corps Commander, also came ashore. Both men expressed delight that the American losses in achieving such a dramatic breakthrough had been so light. The 157th Infantry had suffered only three men killed and nine wounded, the 180th nine killed and forty-nine wounded, and the 179th Infantry—landing on Delta Green—had seen no action at all.

The third of the assault forces, the 36th Infantry Division under General John E. Dahlquist, had the task of landing on the Camel beaches and protecting the right flank of the invasion. The Camel sector ran from the right flank of the 45th Division along the coastline to Théoule-sur-Mer on the Gulf of Napoule, and extended for 20 miles inland along the right bank of the Argens River, taking in Fréjus, Puget-sur-Argens and Le Muy. The coastal zone included the heavily defended beach at the mouth of the Argens. This beach, codenamed Camel Red, was to be reduced at H-plus-6 by land assault from the rear and a frontal attack from the sea. Camel Yellow, on the Rade d'Agay, was also to be attacked from the rear. Camel Green beach was large enough only for an initial landing, while on the extreme right flank Camel Blue Beach was suitable for only a minor landing.

The 2nd and 3rd Battalions, 141st Infantry, went ashore on Camel Green Beach according to schedule, while the 1st Battalion landed on Camel Blue. As the 1st's assault boats emerged from their protective smokescreen, two German antitank guns opened fire on them and scored several direct hits on LCIs in the leading wave. A few seconds later German blockhouses also opened up a murderous fire, most of it coming from the direction of the Anthéor Viaduct. This structure, partly destroyed by RAF Lancasters a few months earlier, was the assault wave's objective and the pivotal point of the attack. Racing through fountains of water hurled up by the enemy shells, the LCIs entered the inlet and grounded in the shallows. The troops lost no time in deploying; although 88mm shells still exploded on the shoreline, the narrow strip of beach was quickly captured. A few minutes later, the enemy gunners shifted their sights to eight amphibious tanks, cruising in towards Camel Green from 4,000 yards offshore. Only one tank was hit, and this beached safely. The others rolled up the beach to pre-determined positions 600 yards from the waterline, where their crews stripped them of their flotation gear.

The 2nd Battalion of the 141st Infantry cleared the right half of Camel Green and then swung north as planned to join the troops of the 1st Battalion, who by this time were swarming on to the Cannes-St Raphaël highway close to the viaduct. By 1000 the Americans were in possession of the whole cape, whose defenders appeared to consist mainly of Polish 'volunteers'.

The 141st's 3rd Battalion cleared the left half of Camel Green, paving a way for the landing of the 143rd Regimental Combat Team between 0945 and 1035. This force moved forward to attack St Raphaël, together with elements of the 141st.

Meanwhile, preparations were going ahead for the delayed landing at H-plus-6 of the 142nd RCT on Camel Red Beach. At 1100, following an intense naval bombardment, minesweepers moved in to clear a lane through the Gulf of Fréjus, but they came under heavy fire from the shore and were forced to retire. The Americans quickly called up air support, and shortly afterwards 93 B-24 Liberators dropped 187 tons of bombs on the enemy defences. Fifteen minutes later the minesweepers tried again. As they passed the mile mark offshore, more shells rained down around them, but they stuck gallantly to their task and swept to within 500 yards of the beach. Naval fire support ships then resumed the barrage, under cover of which two demolition units in scout boats, preceded by a dozen explosive drones, headed for the shore.

In more than 100 assault craft, the 142nd Infantry awaited the signal to land. At two minutes before jump-off time, the rocket ships loosed their missiles on the beach, but still no orders came for the assault to begin. Only three of the radio-controlled drones had exploded as planned, jeopardising the success of the whole operation.

Several minutes after 1400, the troops were still waiting, all the time under heavy fire from camouflaged shore batteries. The Beach Assault Commander radioed a report to Rear-Admiral Spencer Lewis, commanding the invasion in this sector, and recommended that the assault should be re-timed for 1430. Instead, Lewis decided to divert the whole force to Camel Green Beach. This change in plan was relayed by radio and megaphone, and some time later the 142nd Regiment went ashore on Camel Green without loss.

The 142nd's preliminary goal after securing a beachhead was to take Fréjus, and the change of landing place threw the programme behind schedule. On coming ashore at 1532, the 142nd's 1st Battalion made a cross-country dash for Fréjus, closely followed by the 2nd and 3rd Battalions. After an almost superhuman effort, they occupied high ground north-east of the town just before nightfall.

At daylight on D-plus-1, the Americans were fighting in the streets of Fréjus itself, while further along the coast the 143rd RCT was engaged at St Raphaël. By mid-afternoon all enemy resistance had ceased, and all along the invasion area the troops were moving up to their Blue Line objectives. The 142nd Infantry entered Puget late that afternoon, but were temporarily halted by an antitank block beyond the town. During the night, an American paratrooper taken prisoner by the defenders here managed to escape in the middle of an artillery barrage and reported that the Germans had spiked their guns and retreated.

The assault phase was now complete. Shortly before midnight on D-plus-1, General Truscott issued orders to the 3rd, 36th and 45th Divisions to draw up combat and service elements to Le Muy by 1600 the next afternoon to form a provisional armoured group. The VI Corps Commander intended losing no time in exploiting the advantage already gained by the Seventh Army's rapid conquest of the invasion area and was bent on launching a drive north-westward into the interior.

Before the big push could be initiated, however, the Allies had to be in firm possession of the vital ports of Toulon and Marseilles. The task of capturing these objectives had been assigned to the French units of the Seventh Army, which began landing on the beaches already cleared by the VI Corps at 2000 on August 16th. The French force was composed of two corps divided into seven divisions, two of which were armoured; the brunt of the initial fighting was to be borne by the French II Corps, since I Corps was not scheduled to land until D-plus-20. II Corps comprised four divisions: the 1st Infantry and 3rd Algerian Divisions came ashore on D-plus-1, and the 9th Colonial Division disembarked two days later.

The French plan of attack was greatly influenced by the terrain between the beaches and Marseilles. Wooded hills confined movement to two roads running east and west, while the enemy held strongly fortified heights north of Hyères, Toulon and Marseilles. General Patch and the French Commander, de Lattre de Tassigny, expected that the Germans would do everything in their power to delay the Allied exploitation northwards, and it was anticipated that the German High Command would be prepared to sacrifice its 242nd and 244th Divisions in the prolonged defence of both ports. The French also expected to encounter elements of four other divisions, including the mobile 11th Panzer Division.

The French plan hinged on outflanking and encircling the enemy as rapidly as possible. The first objective in this movement was Hyères, which lay some 10 miles from Toulon and a little inland. On August 19th, the 1st Infantry Division advanced towards the town along the coast road. As the French neared Hyères, antitank guns from within the town and larger calibre weapons in the Maurettes Mountains suddenly opened up on them. A regimental combat team, detached from the main body, circled northward to surround the enemy positions in the hills, and by August 20th Hyères had been cut off from the north and east. The isolation of Hyères was completed by the 9th Colonial Division, outflanking the town through thick woods to the north.

Meanwhile, the main body of the 1st Infantry Division had begun the frontal assault. Attacking across the Gapeau River on the morning of August 20th, they were soon held up by heavy fire near the Golf Hotel, where the Germans had a battery of 88mm guns. The French infantry withdrew and two battalions of 105mm and one of 155mm artillery moved up to within 1,000 yards of the enemy positions. In the course of the morning, the French gunners hurled over 1,000 rounds into the town, and in the afternoon Allied warships off the coast added their own bombardment. At 1900, the French infantry fixed bayonets and charged the German positions through heavy small-arms fire. After a fierce hand-to-hand fight, 140 German prisoners were taken. As troops of the 1st Division passed through Hyères on the Toulon road, a motorised battalion assisted men of the FFI in mopping up enemy pockets.

While the battle for Hyères was still raging, the 3rd Algerian Division—having left its assembly area on August 18th and followed an inland route to Méounes—began the encirclement of Toulon. There were four major enemy strongpoints around the town—three on the heights above Toulon and a fourth on the St Mandrier Peninsula south of the city;

all approaches had been blocked by antitank obstacles, pillboxes and minefields, and defensive zones set up with blockhouses and firing trenches protected by wire and mines. Bridges and viaducts were all prepared for demolition. The city was defended by 60 heavy and 100 light guns; heavy artillery included some 16in from the sunken battleship *Provence*. There were also four forts at strategic points within the perimeter of Toulon.

Shortly before the assault, the 3rd Division was strengthened by the arrival of the French Groupe de Commandos, who were soon engaged in fierce fighting on the slopes around Toulon. The assault battalions, the 1st and 3rd Commandos, met strong resistance at the Fort Est du Coudon. The fort's garrison raised a white flag at 1700 hours on August 21st after a three-hour artillery barrage; but as the commandos were scaling the walls by rope to receive the surrender, the Germans signalled by flare for their own artillery to open fire on the fort. French and Germans alike were killed and wounded by the resulting shell-bursts, but the inevitable surrender of the fort was delayed by no more than an hour.

Meanwhile, the 3rd Algerian Division had succeeded in overrunning the three mountain forts north of Toulon. By August 23rd, the town itself was under siege, and the next day it was surrounded on three sides. The German defenders had, as anticipated, received orders to fight to the last man, and the 242nd German Infantry Division offered almost fanatical resistance. It was clear that the occupation of Toulon was going to demand the combined efforts of the French Army, the XII Tactical Air Force and the Western Naval Task Force. On land the French set up a solid ring of fire consisting of six battalions of 155mm guns and six of 105mm tight against the perimeter; these were soon in action, their fire directed with deadly accuracy by observation posts on the heights.

The Air Force concentrated on the peninsula, with the aim of knocking out the installations there and severing the enemy from the mainland. On August 18th and 19th, over 160 B-26 Marauder medium bombers struck at St Mandrier, and on the 20th 121 P-47 Thunderbolts—each carrying two 500lb bombs—joined the air offensive. The bombing was reasonably accurate, but so was the enemy flak; three aircraft were shot down and twenty-five badly damaged.

On August 19th the French warship *Lorraine,* the USS *Nevada* and the USS *Augusta,* operating under cover of a smokescreen, came close inshore to fire 87 rounds on St Mandrier and 124 on Toulon, scoring a direct hit on the old French battleship *Strasbourg*. The naval barrage was stepped up the next day, in tune with the offensive on land, and this time the St Mandrier batteries replied. The German gunners fired sixty shells over a range of 14 miles at the Western Task Force, hitting the FS *Fantasque* and *Georges Leygues* and straddling the USS *Ericsson*. After that the German opposition diminished, and the naval shelling continued for eight successive days with increasing intensity.

The hard-pressed French troops ashore were more than grateful for the naval support. At San Salvador, for example, a battalion of the French Foreign Legion broke through the enemy defences with the help of naval gunfire after a bitter six-hour pitched battle and took 347 prisoners. Naval guns also knocked out pillboxes along the coast which had inflicted severe casualties on the 1st Division. Under cover of a rolling barrage from the warships, troops of both II Corps divisions east of Toulon penetrated the city, and by 1700 on August 23rd advance elements reached the centre. Two tanks under the command of Major Victor Mirkin rolled up to the Military Arsenal in the Le Mourillon sector of Toulon. Mirkin informed the German commander that unless the latter surrendered immediately the warships would pulverise the place. The threat proved sufficient; the commander capitulated, together with 17 officers and 800 men.

On the morning of August 24th, enemy forts and strongpoints surrendered one after the other. At 0900, the Naval Arsenal capitulated with 200 prisoners; Fort Ste Catherine followed suit at 1000; and at 1300 the German garrison at Fort St Louis was ordered to spike its guns. Three more forts surrendered during the afternoon, and by dark organised resistance in the eastern part of Toulon had come to an end. During this day alone, the 1st Infantry Division took over 2,000 prisoners.

In other parts of the city, however, pockets of Germans fought on. The enemy still held the vital port area, against which the French launched a vigorous offensive. A quick result became vital after a radio message was intercepted indicating that the Germans had received orders to destroy all remaining port installations. There was murderous street fighting in the La Colette area of the port as the Germans resisted from house to house. While the French made slow progress here, fighting for every foot of ground, other units pushed on down the Sicie Peninsula, where three forts yielded by noon on August 26th. On that afternoon, the naval barrage reached its climax, with warships closing in to within 5 miles of the St Mandrier fortress. The whole area was shrouded in smoke, punctuated with the glare of fires and explosions, and at 1630 all warships were ordered to cease fire.

At dawn on August 27th, only St Mandrier remained in enemy hands. Later that morning. General Magnan, commanding the 9th Colonial Division, called a halt to the furious artillery barrage directed against the eight surviving German batteries and began surrender negotiations with the garrison. In the end, an agreement was reached and the capitulation became effective at 0600 on August 28th. Among the prisoners taken was Admiral Ruhfus, commander of the Toulon Defences. At 1000, General de Lattre de Tassigny made his formal entry into a Toulon wild with the ecstasy of liberation.

The assault on Marseilles, meanwhile, had started on August 20th, when a group of the 3rd Algerian Division and units of the 1st Armoured Division skirted Toulon to the west and moved against this, France's second largest city. The natural defences of Marseilles were not as formidable as those around Toulon, but there were strongpoints on the heights and forts on two islands in the bay. Added to these were minefields, nets, submarine detectors, heavy coastal guns, 107 antiaircraft guns and several blockships, anchored at strategic points in the harbour ready to be scuttled at short notice.

At first, it seemed as though the French might be able to take the port without a fight. On August 23rd, as three battalions of the 7th Algerian Regiment closed in on Marseilles from different directions, negotiations for surrender were already under way with the German commander, General Schaeffer. These soon broke down, however, and Schaeffer made it plain that his 244th Infantry Division would fight hard for the city. He was as good as his word; the following day, as French troops attacked the perimeter, they were met by a storm of artillery and machine-gun fire from the forts and strongpoints as the Germans clung tenaciously to their positions on the coast. On August 25th, however, the combined weight of the naval and air bombardment began to have its effect, and forty-eight hours later the enemy's plight was becoming desperate—particularly on the two islands off Marseilles, which had received a considerable tonnage of bombs.

The first major strongpoint to fall was on the heights ashore, when it was assaulted from four directions. The garrison hoisted a white flag and surrendered at 1000 on August 26th. Scattered engagements continued in the heart of the city, with house-to-house fighting in the districts of Quatre Chemins, St Joseph and Le Melon. There was a bitter, three-day combat along the waterfront, with Chef-de-Bataillon Roussel leading his Algerians in the hunt for the enemy among the twisting alleyways of La Gavotte and Moulin du Diable.

During the evening of August 27th, a letter from General Schaeffer was delivered to the French General de Monsabert, requesting an audience to discuss surrender terms. At 0700 the next morning, Schaeffer was brought to the Hotel du Quinzième Corps and the talks began. They ended with the surrender of Schaeffer, his staff and 7,000 officers and men.

At 1100 on August 29th, the forces which had taken part in the liberation marched in review past the Commanding General, to the cheers—and tears—of the population. Once more, the strains of the 'Marseillaise', played by the band of the 3rd Algerian Division, echoed through the streets of the city which had given the Anthem birth.

Some of the first German prisoners captured by the Seventh Army on D Day. Many carry inflatable life-belts for their evacuation by sea.

Exploiting their unexpectedly swift penetration inland from the beaches, the Seventh Army thrust forward to threaten the German's second line of defence on the Durance-Verdon rivers. Here troops of the 45th Division pursue the enemy north of Salernes in southern France riding on tanks.

V

After the fall of Toulon and Marseilles, the German forces on the Riviera began a rapid withdrawal up the Rhône Valley, and it was decided that the Allies should lose no time in pursuing them. The French were consequently ordered to drive up the west bank of the Rhône, and the 1st French Infantry and 1st Armoured Divisions crossed the river near Avignon, Tarascon and Arles. These troops fanned out to occupy Nimes and Montpellier, while the 3rd Algerian Infantry Division moved northwards towards Grenoble to relieve elements of the US 45th Division.

The speed of the Seventh Army's advance from the beachheads, meanwhile, had surpassed all expectations. A breakthrough had already been achieved by D-plus-2, and the German Nineteenth Army was in serious danger of being cut in two. The Germans had set up a secondary line of defence about 30-40 miles inland on the Durance-Verdon rivers, but so rapid was the penetration of the 45th Division in this direction that the line was soon threatened. The Allies quickly realised that the invasion had caught the enemy with most of his strength far to the west of the beaches. As late as August 17th, three of the four German divisions west of Marseilles had still not moved into the combat zone; the Allied bombardment had wrecked all but one bridge across the Rhône, and the enemy was also short of vehicles The reserve German division responsible for the defence of the coast east of Toulon had become separated from the 242nd, and by D-plus-1 it was retreating under pressure towards the Italian frontier.

The VI Corps's plan of attack now called for an advance by the 3rd Division, which was to seize and hold positions along the Real Martin River and later continue towards the Rhône Delta. The 45th Division was to assemble at Le Luc and be prepared to push north-west beyond the Maures Mountains. The 36th Division's target was Cannes, whence it was to be ready to advance along the Route Napoleon. To complete the plans, a provisional formation known as Task Force Butler was assembled at Le

Above: After their rapid advance from the invasion beaches in southern France, troops of the 45th Division, Seventh Army, march through Salernes on the heels of the retreating Germans.

Below: Cheering crowds greet Seventh Army reconnaissance troops as they enter Ragusse. On D-Day-plus-3 of their invasion of southern France, they had already penetrated well inland from the beaches.

Muy; this force, commanded by Brigadier-General Frederick B. Butler, set out from Le Muy on August 18th for the Durance River. From there it would drive either on Grenoble or Montélimar.

In the west, the 15th and 30th Regiments of the 3rd Division reached an assembly area near Brignoles on the night of August 17th-18th and took the town the next day, after street fighting which ended in the virtual elimination of the entire 2nd Battalion of the German 757th Infantry Regiment. The 3rd advanced a further 30 miles to Aix-en-Provence, which was reached on August 20th, and an all-out assault on the town was ordered to begin at 0600 the next morning. The 1st Battalion attacked on schedule, with the 2nd Battalion standing by to provide supporting fire, but the Americans encountered only desultory sniper fire in the streets. The main enemy body appeared to have withdrawn, leaving only a small harassing group to delay the advance.

In the centre of the assault area, the 45th Division—comprising the 157th, 179th and 180th Infantry Regiments—made a parallel advance north-westwards. After clearing Barjols on August 19th, the Americans reached the Durance River to find the bridge near St Paul only partly destroyed. The infantry streamed across, encountering only light small-arms fire, and engineers constructed a bridge for the Division's vehicles. Spearheading the American advance as a whole was Task Force Butler, operating between the 45th and 36th Divisions. During their dash northwards to Riez they joined forces with airborne troops in a pitched battle for the German LXII Corps Headquarters, which was overrun with the capture of 400 officers and men.

At Riez, Butler heard that the German 157th Reserve Division was coming down the Grenoble Corridor from the north and already approaching Digne. Seeing an opportunity to encircle the enemy by a flanking manoeuvre, he sent a detachment towards Mézel and Digne, while a larger group with armoured support followed the Durance River. The plan was almost immediately effective, for on the night of August 19th the Americans received the surrender of 600 men of the German garrison at Digne, cut off from the south and west. The main body of Task Force Butler, meanwhile, had crossed the Durance and pressed on to Sisteron. On August 20th, they took the town of Gap together with 1,000 prisoners, a ration dump and a supply dump.

On the right flank of the assault, the 36th Division spread out into the foothills of the Maritime Alps. In Callian, French partisans reinforced a garrison of paratroops which had been trapped and surrounded by the enemy; the town changed hands twice before falling to the Allies. With the right flank secure, the 36th Division drove north-west, preceded by tank destroyers, and made contact with Butler's force. They took Castellane, Draguignan, and Sisteron against only light opposition; the nature of the terrain compelled the Germans to retreat up the Rhône Valley or risk being cut off from their supply routes.

Before D-Day, the German 11th Panzer Division had been stationed near Bordeaux on the Atlantic coast. On August 15th and 16th, air reconnaissance revealed that the entire division, loaded on thirty-three trains, was moving eastward towards the Rhône. Captured enemy field orders disclosed that this division had instructions to hold the eastern side of the triangle formed by the Rhône Delta against the 3rd Division of the Seventh Army, while the four less mobile enemy divisions withdrew along the western edge between Montpellier and Avignon.

Between August 20th and 24th, the German High Command issued five field orders—all captured by the Allies—governing the strategy of the Nineteenth Army's retreat. Field Order No 1, dated August 20th, directed all elements east of the Rhône triangle and south of the Durance to assemble near L'Isle-sur-la-Sorgue. All marches were to be made at night. Soldiers were told to "fight cunningly", and, at the risk of a field court martial, warned against looting and wandering about unarmed. Field Order No 2, dated August 21st, dealt with holding the Rhône triangle to cover the main retreat. The town of Arles was to be strongly defended. Field Order No 3, issued that same day, explained that the rapid expansion of the Allied bridgehead in northern France threatened to sever German communications, so the Nineteenth Army was ordered to disengage itself from the enemy and join the southern wing of the German Army Group B operating in northern and central France. The first specific objective of the retreat was the confluence of the Drôme and Rhône rivers south of Valence. The main emphasis was on keeping open the escape route, though in this order the German troops were also directed to fight to the last man. Field Order No 4 included detailed instructions for the disengagement. The 11th Panzer Division was to continue north to the Cruas Gorge, before Montélimar, while the 198th Infantry was to follow by a series of forced marches. The final Field Order, No 5, covered the last phase of the withdrawal from the Rhône Triangle to the Cruas Gorge.

Reconnaissance flights by XII Tactical Air Command helped to fill in the rest of the picture, revealing the pattern of enemy movements throughout the Rhône Valley. During the first six days after the landings, German rail and road movements tended to conform to the strategic situation, with their divisions swinging eastwards towards the assault beaches. In the Rhône Valley itself, traffic streamed south from Lyons and from Grenoble and there was a general southward movement through the corridor towards the coast. By August 21st, however, the direction of enemy movement had been completely reversed, with convoys nose-to-tail on the northbound route up the valley at Avignon. The Germans were apparently experiencing a critical shortage of fuel; Allied pilots reported sighting many troops being towed on bicycles, with several machines spaced at intervals along a tow rope attached to a troop carrier.

The enemy's retreat was being accelerated by the north-westward drive of the 3rd Division, which reached Arles on August 24th and Avignon the following day. By the 27th, of the eight enemy divisions operating in southern France, two—the 242nd and 244th—were penned hopelessly in Toulon and Marseilles; five were falling back on Montélimar; while the 148th in the Cannes-Nice region and the 157th at Grenoble were retreating towards the Alps and Italy.

While the desperate German retreat continued up the Rhône Valley, the parallel advance by the Americans proceeded up the Grenoble Corridor. The American drive, spearheaded by Task Force Butler, reached Gap on August 20th, closely followed by tactical support from the 36th and 45th Divisions. So well was this move going, in fact, that Truscott could now consider transferring Butler's force west to the Montélimar area. On the evening of August 20th, Butler received orders "to put out reconnaissance forces on the road nets to the north and west, examining the possibility of advancing to the vicinity of Montélimar; to block enemy forces withdrawing up the Rhône Valley from the south; and to make preparations to continue the advance to Grenoble". At 2045 another message was sent from VI Corps: "You will move at first light August 21st with all possible speed to Montélimar. Block all routes of withdrawal up the Rhône Valley in that vicinity. 36th Division follows you."

The main body of Task Force Butler pushed rapidly westward along the valley of the Drôme and by dusk on August 21st elements entered the Rhône Valley. No contact was made with the enemy until the vanguard of Butler's men met a northbound convoy of thirty German vehicles; they ripped straight through it, destroying several trucks and causing some casualties. Butler reached the high ground overlooking the valley and set up his command post at Marsanne.

In the evening of August 22nd, the 36th Division reached Grenoble, with the 143rd Infantry Regiment leading the way. While the 142nd Infantry held road-blocks north and east of Gap, the 141st Regimental Combat Team with the 141st and 977th Field Artillery Battalions were transferred to the zone held by Task Force Butler, in readiness for the coming assault on Montélimar.

The town of Montélimar was a key communications centre, which made

In pursuit of the retreating Germans, the 3rd
Division drove north-west into France from
the beaches. Nine days after their landing
they were being greeted by cheering crowds at
Salon on the road to Avignon.

it imperative for the Americans to try to block the enemy retreat at this point. The task of seizing the town was assigned to the 141st Infantry Regiment, which was scheduled to attack from the north and north-east on the afternoon of August 23rd, supported by a platoon of tank destroyers and one of tanks. The latter, however, failed to turn up, and when the advance began it was without armoured support. The Americans were halted by heavy artillery fire while still some distance from the town, and a group of French Maquisards which also took part in the attack was almost annihilated.

The Allied failure to take Montélimar meant that the Germans were still free to move northward along Highway 7 and eastward along the Roubion River, which ran through the town and along which the Americans as yet had only a token force for flank protection. Since August 21st, however, Highway 7 had been under continual and deadly accurate air attack and artillery fire, and the Germans were suffering such casualties that they would soon be forced to consider an alternative escape route. The Americans consequently built up their forces along the Roubion River line as rapidly as possible; if they could deny this escape route to the Germans, it would mean that the latter would have to go on using Highway 7, running the gauntlet of intense Allied fire.

At 1400 on August 24th, the 36th Division issued its orders. The main line of resistance was to follow the northern bank of the Roubion, facing south to prevent the enemy from breaking out. Field artillery battalions were to lay down fire on the roads leading into the Rhône Valley and cover the Bordeaux-Crest route.

On August 24th, however, a copy of the 36th's orders fell into the hands of the enemy. Not only were the Germans forewarned of Allied plans to trap them, but the content of the orders indicated that Bonlieu was the weakest point in the American line. In front of this village, a composite company of the 111th Engineer Battalion lay spread out over an area 3,000 yards long, and at 1600 on August 25th German troops, supported by two tanks, launched an attack there. Covered by fire from the tanks, they crossed the Roubion and forced the Americans back several hundred yards. Soon afterwards, a second assault completely cut the Roubion defence line. More German troops crowded through the gap, and their breakthrough at Bonlieu cut all contact between the 141st and 142nd Regiments. The Americans quickly rushed up reinforcements, relieving the engineer company, and within forty-eight hours the original main line of resistance had been restored by the 1st Battalions of the 143rd and 142nd Infantry. The Americans did not know how many Germans had slipped through the gap, but interrogation of prisoners revealed that they formed part of the 11th Panzer and 198th Infantry Divisions.

Meanwhile, blocking Highway 7 had become a top priority task, but two attempts to set up a road-block by Task Force Butler and the 141st Infantry were repulsed on August 25th. Later in the day, the 141st had another try, this block being protected by a platoon of infantry, six tank destroyers and three tanks, but again the Germans succeeded in breaking through.

It was the American artillery which, in the end, smashed the flow of enemy traffic northwards along Highway 7. Beginning at 0630 on August 27th, the artillery battalions laid a furious barrage along the road, which was soon obscured by the smoke of burning vehicles. By 2130, the 1st Battalion of the 141st Infantry reported that a road-block had been created by the wrecked enemy vehicles themselves, and that tanks and motor transport were trying to by-pass the barrier to reach the Drôme River. The Americans did not have enough ammunition to achieve as much damage as they might have done, and what rounds were available were constantly being shifted about between units to hit the best targets. On the 27th, the 133rd Field Artillery Battalion scored two direct hits on a train of fifty-five cars in the Rhône Valley, and two other trains—blocked by the wreckage—were also hit. The three trains were eventually captured together with their contents, which included five large railway guns.

Highway 86, on the west bank of the Rhône—with sharp curves in the road clinging to the sides of steep crags—offered a less desirable escape route than Highway 7, but as pressure built up against them the enemy were forced to use it. As late as August 27th-28th, two bridges across the Rhône were still being used by the Germans, and their location enabled some of the enemy traffic to avoid the more direct fire of the American artillery. The failure to deny the enemy the use of these two bridges enabled them to exploit this alternative route to the fullest advantage.

It was not until the US 3rd Division reached Montélimar from the south that the 141st Regiment was able to occupy the surrounding high ground and drive south across the Roubion River to smash remaining enemy resistance in the area. The town was occupied by American forces the same day.

The Drôme River was now the last barrier in the German retreat to Lyons, and to close their only route across the river air strikes were called down by the Americans. On August 25th, the last two bridges across the river were knocked out by artillery and aircraft, but the Germans made use of four fording sites near Highway 7. Enemy tanks crossed these on railroad sleepers laid on top of crushed stone and gravel, and heavy equipment was winched across. On August 27th, however, with the river still at low level, a sudden thunderstorm broke in the mountains. A torrent of water flooded down the river bed, and for several hours the enemy convoys were immobilised on the south bank. Artillery and aircraft took their toll before the columns were able to get on the move once more.

On August 27th, American artillery assembled in strength in an all-out effort to smash the enemy's northward movement up the Rhône Valley. The 'Long Toms' of the 977th Field Artillery Battalion were sighted on the Drôme crossings near the river's confluence with the Rhône. These long-range weapons destroyed the railroad bridge, highway bridge and one of the major fords which the Germans were using. On August 28th, the artillery shifted northwards to intercept the convoys of foliage-camouflaged enemy traffic trying to get through the narrow bottleneck on the Drôme. The 132nd Field Artillery Battalion alone caused the destruction or abandonment of 500 vehicles and 50 artillery pieces.

The final drive into Montélimar by the 3rd Division on August 28th caught only the German rearguard, and by the end of the day all enemy resistance in the town had ceased. By this time, the Germans had succeeded in getting most of the Nineteenth Army clear, but they left a litter of abandoned equipment in their wake. Although the High Command could claim success in breaking out of the Montélimar trap, the Americans still had another chance to intercept them before they reached the Belfort Gap. The Seventh Army's Field Order No 4, dated August 28th, directed that every attempt should be made to destroy the Nineteenth Army before it managed to withdraw beyond the Rhine. The French Army B was to proceed along the west bank of the Rhône and help to take Lyons, while VI Corps advanced on the Lyons-Beaune-Dijon axis.

Dijon, however, lay due west of the entrance to the Belfort Gap, and many enemy elements were expected to turn eastward at Lyons to take the most direct route to the Gap and the Rhine. If the Seventh Army could reach Dijon quickly enough to join Allied forces striking south-eastward from Normandy, much of the Nineteenth Army would be cut off west of the Rhine.

The Americans maintained close reconnaissance contact with the retreating Germans, and the 45th Division was ordered to push north-west from Grenoble to cut across the axis connecting Lyons with the Swiss border. The 36th Division was to continue northward towards Lyons, while the 3rd Division mopped up enemy units around Montélimar. Task Force Butler was to be disbanded after capturing Loriol, on the Drôme.

The main manoeuvring element for this shearing operation of the Seventh Army was the 179th Infantry Regiment of the 45th Division. Their advance patrols spread out beyond Grenoble, and by August 27th they had taken the town of Bourgoin, midway between Grenoble and Lyons. They then occupied Pont D'Ain, cutting off Lyons from the north-east, and set up blocks on all roads radiating east from Lyons, so that the direction of the general German retreat was forced further northward.

There still remained elements of five German divisions, all using the upper Rhône Valley as an escape route. The 716th Division and part of the 189th had avoided the Montélimar trap by racing northwards along the west bank of the Rhône, and by August 27th the bulk of the 11th Panzer Division, which had been covering the retreat, had crossed the Drôme and was well on its way to Lyons. The slower infantry divisions, however, still lagged south of the city as late as August 30th.

The destruction of mobile equipment slowed down the rate of the German retreat. Half-tracks, lorries and all the other impedimenta of a modern army lay burnt out or wrecked along the main highways and minor routes. On August 30th, 200 enemy vehicles—three-quarters of them horse-drawn—were sighted crossing the Isère River. In his haste to clear Lyons, the enemy was driving his columns by day and night, and the convoys presented good targets to Allied air power and the guerrilla bands of the FFI.

In their retreat from southern France, the Germans not only protected their withdrawal from Lyons, but also managed to round the Swiss frontier to the north-east of the town by the clever use of armour in screening their turning movement. By using the Swiss border as a hinge and guarding their extreme western flank against encirclement, they were ultimately able to swing all their columns north-eastward towards the Belfort Gap. Whether they would reach the Gap before they were cut to pieces, however, was a different matter; the cost of the retreat so far had been high. The Nineteenth Army had lost at least 2,500 vehicles, 80 artillery pieces and 5 large-calibre railway guns at the hands of the US Field Artillery Battalions alone, while over 57,000 men had been taken prisoner. The Seventh Army's casualties during the same period totalled 2,733 killed, wounded or missing.

The growing speed of the westward advance gave rise to some problems in the east, where a constantly-lengthening flank had to be protected. General Patch was aware that the German 148th Reserve Division, which had retreated across the Italian border, was in a good position to harass the Seventh Army's right flank, while a major counter-attack by strong German forces through the Alpine passes was not out of the question.

Two of the early Allied objectives on the eastern flank were Cannes and Nice, the liberation of which was of special significance to the French. The capture of Cannes, where the enemy held strongly-fortified heights, was assigned to the 509th Parachute Battalion and the 463rd Parachute Field Artillery Battalion, with the 509th's northern flank secured by the 551st

Parachute Infantry Battalion. Most of the German strongpoints were knocked out by naval gunfire, but entry into the city was delayed until a suitable crossing could be constructed over the Siagne River. Engineers worked all night on August 23rd-24th, building a ford and clearing minefields, and before their task was finished reconnaissance patrols returned with the news that Cannes was clear of the enemy. At 1700 on August 24th, the 509th made its triumphal entry. Forty-eight hours later, the 509th pushed northwards, sending out patrols to St Laurent du Var on the west bank of the Var River. Here they met some FFI who had passed through the German lines; the Frenchmen told them that the Var Valley had been cleared by the enemy and that Nice was also clear. The city was entered by the 509th Combat Team on the 30th.

The Allies were forbidden to enter the principality of Monaco unless it was known to be occupied by the enemy. If that were the case, the Seventh Army would have to cross the frontier to secure its eastern flank. Patrols reconnoitred the French-Monaco border, but made no contact with the enemy, and soon afterwards the FFI confirmed that Monte Carlo was free of Germans. An enemy strongpoint nearby, however, held out for several days despite heavy shelling by Allied naval forces; the defenders were dislodged by the 1st Battalion of the 551st Parachute Infantry and subsequently retreated eastward towards La Roche.

While the paratroops were approaching Cannes, the 1st Special Service Force prepared to attack Grasse, and on August 24th the 517th Parachute Regimental Combat Team took St Vallier. The 517th was also responsible for maintaining contact with VI Corps near Digne, further to the north-west, a task that was considerably eased by the capture of enemy fuel for use by the mobile patrols.

On August 28th, the 550th Airborne Infantry Battalion, reinforced by artillery, mortars and tank destroyers, received orders to make for the Larche Pass in the Alps, behind which intelligence had reported a large assembly of enemy troops; it was feared that a big enemy infiltration might be imminent. An American motorised patrol reported that the Germans were in the process of occupying strategic passes in the mountains, including Larche, to improve their defensive position in the Maritime and Basses Alps. The 550th Combat Team arrived in the area on the 29th, their strength augmented by the FFI and the Inter-Allied Mission—special airborne forces which had been dropped weeks before D-Day—and soon afterwards a large air strike was called down on the approaches to the pass from the Italian side. After that, there was no sign of any further offensive action by the enemy.

With the threat here apparently eliminated, the eastern flank of the

Seventh Army was secure. In the west, the Allied drive could continue towards its ultimate goal—the meeting between the invasion forces of 'Dragoon' and 'Overlord'.

VI

By the end of August, the victorious Seventh Army had completed the liberation of southern France and was closing on Lyons. On the west bank of the Rhône below the town, units of French Army B pushed the enemy northwards, while French reconnaissance groups advanced along the Mediterranean coast close to the Spanish border. In the north, VI Corps units had already crossed the Rhône where it flowed into Lyons from the high Alps to the east of the city, and were now in action to the north-east. The US Third Army, meanwhile, was striking east, north-east and south-east from Paris; the whole of the German forces south of the Loire and west of the Rhône-Saône rivers faced total isolation as the spearheads of the Third and Seventh Armies approached one another. By August 25th, plans for the link-up of 'Overlord' and 'Dragoon' were well advanced, and the Mediterranean phase of Seventh Army operations began to draw to a close as the European phase opened.

On August 29th, Patch revealed that his tactical plans envisaged a high speed dash to Lyons by VI Corps from Valence and Grenoble, the advance subsequently continuing on the Lyons-Beaune-Dijon axis. After the capture of Lyons, VI Corps was to regroup for operations on the line Autun-Dijon-Langres with the object of making contact with Patton's Third US Army. With Lyons in Allied hands, the Seventh Army would be in a position to push on rapidly in the hope of rolling up the German Nineteenth Army and driving the remnants out of France. In a simultaneous move, the French would advance on the right flank as far as the Italian and Swiss frontiers.

Captured documents and the statements of prisoners-of-war revealed that the Germans intended to use Lyons as the initial assembly point for an orderly withdrawal north-eastwards to the frontiers of Germany itself; this would be carried out along the main Lyons-Dijon highway under cover of screening actions to the south.

67

The bulk of the German Nineteenth Army passed through the Montélimar trap on August 28th. Under continual shelling and air attack, the battered remnants went on withdrawing up the Rhône valley to Lyons, whence German forces were already moving in a steady stream towards the Belfort Gap and the Vosges. On September 1st, the Germans pouring through the Lyons-Dijon funnel represented all that remained of the occupation forces in southern France. These included, in addition to the units which were in direct contact with the Seventh Army, substantial forces which had been concentrated in the Loire River-Bordeaux-Toulouse-Vichy area. Desperately trying to reach safety in the east before being cut off by the approaching junction of the Third and Seventh US Armies were also two divisions of the German First Army, the 16th and 159th, as well as the Nineteenth Army's 716th Division which was retreating from the west bank of the Rhône.

South of Lyons, an estimated 8,730 combat troops still opposed the Seventh Army, but captured German mail revealed that enemy morale was rapidly disintegrating. In some cases outright panic began to spread as the German troops realised that their only hope was to fight their way through to link-up with their forces in the north, where a defensive line could be established.

The end of August found major elements of the Seventh Army forming a semi-circle north-east of Lyons around the retreating enemy columns. Over on the western side of the arc, the newly organised French II Corps was also advancing rapidly on Lyons from west of the Rhône. All three American divisions were closing in for the kill. The 3rd Division mopped up around Montélimar and then pushed on to Voiron, north of Grenoble, for a drive north-westwards to Lyons, while the 36th Division continued the chase up the Rhône valley; by September 1st it was at Vienne, due south of the threatened city. The 45th Division was close to the 3rd, to the east.

Since Lyons—France's third city and an important industrial centre, as well as a focus for internal waterways, railroads and highways—was so vital a link in the German line of withdrawal, Allied Intelligence had been certain that the enemy would defend it, if only for a limited time. However, enemy documents captured on September 1st showed that no attempt would in fact be made to hold the city; the Germans had decided to abandon the whole of the Lyons-Dijon-Besançon defensive triangle and evacuate Lyons as soon as they were ready to continue their northerly withdrawal.

The way was now clear for a high-speed dash to Lyons by the 36th Division, as directed in a VI Corps Field Order of August 31st. The 45th

Division would cover the Corps's right flank, and the 3rd Division could be called upon to support either the 36th or 45th as required. Support was also anticipated from the French Forces of the Interior. There were some 4,000 FFI irregulars in the area, and the Resistance had drawn up several plans for harassing the enemy; one involved seizing tram-cars from a depot on the west bank of the Saône and blocking the narrow streets of the city with them to hamper the German withdrawal. In fact the FFI had expressed a strong desire to liberate Lyons entirely on their own initiative, but General de Gaulle's military representatives warned their leaders against precipitate action and this scheme was abandoned. The FFI were subsequently ordered to make contact with the Allied columns approaching the outskirts of the city, and although they were to harass the enemy at every opportunity they were not to engage the Germans openly.

German detachments manning road-blocks in the path of the American forces advancing on Lyons east of the Rhône offered no serious opposition, falling back as rapidly as possible on the city. Once again, only slight opposition was encountered when, in the afternoon of September 1st, the 142nd Infantry of the 36th Division reached the hills overlooking Lyons and moved down to take key positions east and south-east of the city.

At 1130 on September 2nd, General Dahlquist ordered a reconnaissance patrol to investigate reports that Lyons had already been evacuated. Early that afternoon, it was confirmed that the Germans had fallen back as far as the Rhône, to a position from which their artillery still commanded the approaches to the city.

At 1700, General Butler ordered the 36th Division not to enter Lyons; instead, patrols were to be sent out to maintain contact with the FFI and French Army B, which were approaching from the west. This was a gentlemanly gesture on Butler's part; while the Americans waited on the outskirts of Lyons, French troops marched in and claimed the honour of liberating the city, although by this time only a few isolated pockets of German troops remained.

On the west bank of the Rhône, the French II Corps drove on steadily through light resistance and on September 2nd its forward units also reached the outskirts of Lyons. The following day the 1st French Infantry Division entered the city and deployed along its entire perimeter west of the rivers.

While the French II Corps and the US 36th Division were thus involved, the 45th Division had made contact with the enemy to the north-east. On September 1st, about 1,000 German troops supported by tanks and self-propelled guns of the 11th Panzer Division smashed through an Allied road-block and launched a furious attack on the 179th Infantry, which was holding a road junction at Meximieux. The first assault was beaten off, but another developed from the south and a savage battle flared up around the railway station, where the Americans had established their main defence. The Germans made repeated attempts to batter a hole in the defences with their tanks; at one point, several erupted from the cover of the woods and raced across the railroad into the town before the Americans could bring their artillery to bear on them. A few minutes later, however, five of the tanks came speeding down the main street, and the American gunners saw their chance. Four of the Panzers were quickly knocked out by tank destroyers; two of the crews baled out and were killed or captured. The remaining tank got away. In the afternoon, eight more tanks came clattering down the highway from Lyons, but these were dealt with by artillery fire and by groups of FFI wielding bazookas and Molotov cocktails.

As darkness fell, the Germans began to withdraw, leaving many dead scattered in the light of the burning tanks. In all the enemy lost 350 men killed and wounded, with a further 41 taken prisoner. Considering the fury of the action, Allied losses were extremely light; the 1st Battalion of the 179th, which had been in the thick of the battle, reported only eleven casualties during the day.

The rapid occupation of Lyons and the unexpected speed of the German withdrawal brought about a change in the original plan for regrouping the Seventh Army at this stage. Their assigned mission—to land in southern France, take Toulon and Marseilles and probe northwards towards Lyons and Vichy—had been completed, although the Americans had not yet formally entered the last-named town, and it was consequently decided to continue the pursuit of the enemy and effect a link-up with the Third Army much sooner than planned.

Two possible escape routes out of France lay open to the Germans. They could go up the Saône Valley to Châlon-sur-Saône, then north to Dijon, beyond to Chaumont or Épinal, and so on to Nancy; this route would keep them clear of the Vosges mountains to the east and afford good road and rail communications. It would also place the Doubs and Saône Rivers between them and the advancing Seventh Army. The big snag was that this route throughout its length was already being threatened by the advance of the US Third Army towards Nancy. The alternative route followed the valley of the Doubs north-east of Châlon-sur-Saône, passing between the Alps and Vosges and extending north-east from Dole through Besançon and Baume-les-Dames towards Montbéliard. From there the main lines of communication passed through the Belfort Gap to Mulhouse and the Rhine. This route was more direct than the first, and here too the Germans could use the natural obstacle of the Doubs to good advantage as they withdrew along its north-west bank. Once they were past Besançon, the Alps and neutral Switzerland would cover their southern flank and the Vosges their northern; they would then have the choice either of defending the line of the Vosges or escaping across the Rhine.

In the early hours of September 3rd, a special officer courier arrived at the command post of the Seventh Army with an urgent message from General Truscott. The VI Corps commander stated that the Germans were in full retreat and greatly disorganised, and that delaying actions at advantageous defensive positions were the only opposition to be expected. In addition, the Corps was in contact with elements of the 11th Panzer Division in the Bourg area and had destroyed fifteen enemy tanks the previous day. Truscott intended to give the enemy no respite; he wanted VI Corps to drive after them hard and fast along the Lons-Le Saunier-Besançon-Belfort axis to try to prevent their escape into Germany.

After a staff conference, VI Corps was authorised to continue the "relentless pursuit" of the enemy, and Truscott lost no time in executing his new orders. On the morning of September 3rd, the 117th Cavalry Reconnaissance Squadron penetrated as far as Bourg-en-Bresse, due west of Geneva—but the Americans were soon to learn to their cost that on this occasion they had advanced too far and too fast. Soon after nightfall, units of the 11th Panzer Division—heading northwards at top speed after the skirmish at Meximieux—also roared into Bourg-en-Bresse, taking the 117th completely by surprise. In the confused, violent battle that followed 'B' Troop of the 117th was wiped out almost to a man. The Americans also lost twenty 5cwt trucks, fifteen armoured cars and two light tanks before they managed to extricate themselves, although they were able to inflict significant casualties on the enemy.

The next day, the 45th Division occupied Bourg-on-Bresse and drove on towards the Doubs after a brief respite. The renewed advance, however, quickly became bogged down; not only were there formidable logistic problems to be overcome—with Lyons 70 miles to the rear and the main Allied supply depots still on the beaches, over 250 miles away—but the enemy had blown many bridges, making necessary long detours over muddy, barely negotiable tracks.

The Germans planned to make a stand on the Doubs River and to hold Besancon until mid-September in the hope that this would allow sufficient time for their forces in the Dijon area to withdraw through the Belfort Gap. Besançon was an almost ideal defensive position. A fortress built by nature and improved over the centuries by generations of military engineers, the industrial heart of the city was guarded by a great loop in the river, while the main approaches were dominated by one major fort, La

Citadelle, and four minor ones. Dating from the 17th century, these thick-walled, moated structures were capable of withstanding the heaviest artillery fire and air bombardment. Other, smaller forts were situated at key positions elsewhere in the city; manning the whole defensive system, the Germans had an estimated 3,000 troops.

Although the American advance was beginning to lose momentum, it was nevertheless still rapid enough to throw the whole German withdrawal plan into jeopardy. By September 5th, the bulk of VI Corps was concentrated south-east of the city; the 3rd Division had moved up to the centre of the VI Corps line to launch an attack from the south, while the 36th Division moved round to the north-west and the 45th to the north-east.

While the 3rd Division closed in and occupied high ground on three sides of Besançon, the 7th Infantry Regiment captured a vital bridge on the left and a battalion of the 30th Infantry crossed swamp land to the north-east of the city, taking a village and a fort. From this vantage point, tanks, tank destroyers and artillery were able to pour a withering fire into the columns of enemy vehicles struggling to escape along the Belfort road. As darkness fell, a 2-mile stretch of the route was lit up by a lurid firework display of flares, exploding ammunition and igniting fuel tanks as the American shells found their targets.

During the night of September 6th/7th, a battalion of the 15th Infantry took Fort Fontain, and the following afternoon Fort Tousey and Fort Trois Châtels fell to the 30th Regiment in rapid succession. Fifty-four Germans were taken prisoner; the remainder made a break for La Citadelle, some being picked off by small-arms fire as they ran.

With the four minor forts out of action, the Americans could now bring up their artillery for a close-range bombardment of La Citadelle itself. As the smoke and dust drifted slowly away at the end of the non-stop, two-hour shelling, the American infantry crossed the moat and prepared to launch the final assault on the battered walls with scaling ladders. But the 250 defenders of La Citadelle had had enough; they offered only token resistance before surrendering.

While the 3rd Division occupied Besançon, the 36th Division also clashed with the enemy as it probed for river crossings over the Doubs 30 miles to the south-west. North-west of Besançon, the 143rd Infantry—engaged in mopping up pockets of enemy troops—captured intact a big fuel dump containing 177,500 gallons of gasoline and 4,000 gallons of alcohol. In view of the Seventh Army's critical shortage of motor fuel, the find could hardly have been more precious.

After nearly a month of fast pursuit, however, the Seventh Army's war of rapid movement was coming to an end. The advance now slowed down significantly as summer gave way to autumn; the streams swelled, the ground grew too soft for cross-country dashes with armoured vehicles. The Americans were forced to plod mile after mile through hills and woodland in the face of an enemy whose alertness was constantly growing. The initial panic was over; the Germans were re-grouping and would fight hard at a time and place of their own choosing.

Although thousands of prisoners had been taken and vast tracts of territory liberated, the German High Command had nevertheless been able to extricate a considerable portion of its forces from the Allied trap in southern France; an estimated 100,000 enemy troops were now in sight of the Rhine and temporary safety; and, as Truscott explained to VI Corps, those who escaped now would turn and fight sooner or later. On September 8th, he issued the following order:

"The purpose of this operation is to destroy by killing or capturing the maximum number of enemy formations. Therefore the following should be observed:

a. Make every effort to entrap enemy formations, regardless of size. Long-range fire, especially artillery, will merely warn and cause a change in direction.

b. All units, but especially battalions and lower units, must be kept well in hand. Commanders of all ranks must avoid wide dispersion and consequent lack of control.

c. Tanks must accompany leading infantry elements and tank destroyers must accompany leading tanks. All must be supported by artillery emplaced well forward.

d. Reconnaissance must be continuous and thorough—foot elements to a distance of 5 miles, motor elements to contact with the enemy.

e. Contact once gained must be maintained. The enemy must not be allowed to escape.

f Every attack must be pressed with the utmost vigor. Be vicious. Seek to kill and destroy."

When this directive reached the front-line units, the chances of sustaining an effective pursuit and of bringing about an early junction of the Normandy and Riviera invasion forces still appeared highly promising. Truscott's VI Corps had reached the Doubs; General Monsabert's French II Corps was pushing steadily along the west banks of the Rhône and Saône towards the eagerly-awaited link-up with the US Third Army, at the same time covering the left flank of the advance, and the French I Corps under General Bethouart had moved north, protecting the right flank. By

September 6th, Bethouart had reached a point only 10 miles short of Montbéliard and 20 miles from the vital Belfort Gap, while the French II Corps was 70 miles north of Lyons. Tactical air power played a vital part in supporting the Allied advance; on September 3rd, for example, Allied fighter-bombers annihilated an entire convoy of 300 enemy horse-drawn vehicles in a single lightning air strike north of Châlon. That same day the French II Corps took Villefranche, and with it 2,400 prisoners.

On September 7th the French occupied Châlon-sur-Saône and pressed on towards Beaune with the co-operation of the FFI. The enemy attempted a counter-attack on the French rear near Chagny, but this was beaten off and the Germans lost 400 dead. Despite deteriorating conditions of terrain, the pace was terrific now, as advanced French elements raced on to meet the XV Corps of the Third Army. Only 25 miles separated the French from Dijon; the capture of this city would not only cut off the main enemy escape route, but also outflank the Doubs line.

On September 9th, French armoured elements hit the midway mark between Beaune and Dijon. Once more, the Germans tried desperately to stem the advance, and once more they received a severe mauling, with 300 men killed and 300 vehicles destroyed. Excitement now ran at fever pitch as the 1st French Armoured Division swept on to Dijon, the capital of Burgundy, and liberated the town on September 10th. The Germans had not tried to defend it. On their right flank, the French made contact with the 117th Cavalry of VI Corps at Auxonne, creating a continuous army front.

Then came the historic moment. During the night of September 10th/11th, an armoured reconnaissance group operating west of Dijon joined hands with a patrol from the 2nd French Armoured Division of the US Third Army at Sombernon.

It was still too early to say whether the trap was completely closed, although large enemy forces were reported still to be west of Dijon. However, the Allies would not have to wait long before learning the full extent of their success.

The next day, September 11th, French II Corps's armoured spearhead thrust on towards Langres, while the infantry set up a static defence line west of Dijon and prepared to meet any German attempt to break out of the trap. Reconnaissance groups probed the countryside north-west of the Dijon-Langres highway. Things were happening fast; at 0700 on September 12th, advance elements of the 1st French Infantry Division linked in force with a regiment of the 2nd French Armoured Division from Paris near Châtillon-sur-Seine, and shortly afterwards came the news that the German forces west of the Loire—some 18,000 men, including three

Generals and an Admiral—had agreed to surrender to the American General commanding Tours.

So, less than a month after the start of Operation 'Dragoon', the two Allied armies had succeeded in cementing a continuous front stretching in a great arc from the English Channel to the hills and forests of eastern France. With the right—or eastern—flank of the Seventh Army checked by the German defence of the Belfort Gap, the front swung from an east-west to a north-south axis.

The momentum of the advance was running down, but stiffening enemy resistance could not prevent the Allied capture of Vesoul, blocking the last direct escape route to Belfort in the VI Corps zone. Lure and Luxeuil also fell and the Americans footslogged on, marching through drenching autumn rain, swinging once more towards the east and the Moselle.

VII

There could be no question that the Seventh Army's advance northwards from the Riviera in the summer of 1944 had been brilliantly executed. At the same time, there was no escaping the fact that both the Americans and French had not encountered anything like the stiff resistance expected. It was not until the latter part of September that the Allied advance met an organised foe, strongly entrenched behind a prepared defensive line. The Germans now had the advantage of considerably shorter lines of supply and communication; they were continuing to receive substantial reinforcements, and they held ground highly favourable for defensive action.

General Patch anticipated that the enemy's plans would be divided into four main phases: delaying actions at intervals between the Doubs and Moselle rivers, a defence of the western approaches to the Vosges, a defence of the reverse slopes overlooking the Rhine and—last and most formidable of all—a defence of the east bank of the Rhine itself.

The Vosges are divided into two chains, the High and Low Vosges, with the Saverne Gap separating the two. At the southern end of the High Vosges is the Belfort Gap, the main avenue of approach to the Plain of Alsace. Épinal on the Moselle is pivot centre of the High Vosges region and two major routes from this town pass through the mountains, one to Strasbourg and the Rhine and the other to Colmar and the Alsace Plain.

Before VI Corps could reach the Vosges, it had to cross the Moselle. In many places—such as at Épinal, where it was 80ft across and flanked by sheer 20ft banks—the river presented a formidable obstacle. There were easier crossing points above and below the town, and it was here that the Germans were concentrating some of their heaviest defences. There was evidence of German resistance all along the Belfort-Vosges line; every barracks in Alsace and Baden was crammed to overflowing with troops, and strong concentrations of artillery were being assembled at Épinal and other garrisons in north-eastern France. The Germans were breaking their backs to throw up fortifications along the whole crest of the Vosges and were building up stockpiles of arms and ammunition at strategic points. By September 19th, VI Corps realised all too well that there was a stiff fight ahead of it. The Vosges, backed by the Siegfried Line, would be the toughest nut in the enemy's long defensive line from the North Sea to the Swiss border.

On September 20th, the 45th Division moved into positions facing the Moselle opposite Épinal. Thus placed they were between the 36th Division and the XV Corps of the US Third Army, forming the Seventh Army's left flank. The Seventh now occupied a zone about 12 miles wide, separated to the north-east by three towns from the Third Army and by three more towns from the First French Army to the south-east.

Patrols indicated that the Germans were withdrawing beyond the Moselle, and on September 20th units of VI Corps stood ready to resume the assault. At 1900, Truscott issued orders detailing the plan of advance. The 45th Division on the left was to seize Épinal and secure a crossing, then drive north-east to force open the Saverne Gap; the 36th Division in the centre was to cross in the Éloyes area and seize St Die near the Saales Pass. Meanwhile the 3rd Division was to cross the river in the Rupt area, advancing to take Gerardmer near the Schlucht Pass. After reaching these various objectives, VI Corps would thrust on through the Saverne Gap towards Strasbourg.

The initial move was to be made by the 36th Division, which had been assembling river-crossing equipment since September 18th. By the night of the 20th/21st, the Division had a total of sixty-five assault craft, and twenty-five DUKWs were en route. Engineers had assembled an armoured treadway and an infantry support bridge.

The 141st Infantry Regiment was to spearhead the assault, crossing near Éloyes and securing a bridgehead. The men moved off towards the river through dense woodland, guided by the sixty-year-old Mayor of a local village—a retired naval officer. He had often visited his daughter in Éloyes, taking short-cuts to save a mile or two, and in fact was one of the very few people in the area who could traverse the forest unerringly away from the beaten track.

Nevertheless, it was hard going; the night was pitch dark and showery, which made movement through the trees even more difficult. At 0030 on September 21st, the 131st and 155th Field Artillery Battalions opened fire on positions across the river, and at 0500 radio silence was broken to determine the location of the 141st Infantry's 2nd Battalion. Meanwhile, the 1st and 3rd Battalions emerged from the trees and pushed on across the river valley towards the crossing point, the men moving like wraiths through a thick fog which muffled all sounds into an uncanny silence once the roar of artillery fire had died away.

The 1st Battalion slipped across the Moselle just after 0700 and were quickly in action on the other side. At 0914, they called for extra mortar bombs and grenades, and at 0944 the 3rd Battalion was ordered across in support. Leading two platoons of 'I' Company, the commander of the 3rd Battalion attempted to cross the river some distance south of the spot where the 1st had gone over. The reason for his choice was that the banks of the first crossing place were devoid of cover for several hundred yards on both sides of the Moselle, and that the dense fog which had shielded the 1st Battalion was now rapidly dispersing.

At first, everything seemed to go well. Two platoons crossed the river without incident and began to move slowly up the slope on the other side. The first was halfway up when all hell broke loose. From a thickly wooded hill at the top of the slope, a storm of machine-gun fire scythed through the mist, cutting down the infantry before they had a chance to react. The whole of the leading platoon was wiped out in the first few seconds, and the other suffered 50 per cent casualties before it managed to struggle back across the river. The battalion commander was reported missing and his S-3 killed in action.

After this disaster, the remainder of the 3rd Battalion moved north to the original ford, and General Dahlquist ordered Colonel Steele to take command. Meanwhile, the 2nd Battalion had occupied the half of Éloyes laying on the west bank of the Moselle, but the three bridges spanning the swiftly flowing river had been blown and enemy machine-guns covered the river from emplacements in the eastern part of the town.

At 1515 that afternoon, the 143rd Regimental Combat Team began crossing the river to the south, with the object of attacking Éloyes from the south-east, encountering only sporadic small-arms fire as they did so. Shortly before nightfall, the 3rd Battalion of the 143rd captured Hill 783, overlooking the town, while to the south-east the 1st Battalion attacked Hill 605 in the face of intense artillery, mortar and machine-gun fire.

The enemy shelled the American positions steadily throughout the night of September 21st/22nd, the damp fog making it impossible to locate their gun positions. Shortly before dawn, the fog also enabled a company of Germans to infiltrate into the 1st Battalion's lines from Hill 605 and a savage hand-to-hand fight raged before they were beaten off. During the afternoon of the 22nd, the 143rd Regiment launched an all-out attack on Éloyes and occupied it after five hours of bitter street fighting. While the 141st and 143rd consolidated the bridgehead, the 142nd occupied Remiremont, west of the river.

Above: On 22nd September, the 3rd
Battalion of the 157th Infantry Regiment
spearheaded the 45th Divisions drive across
the Moselle river towards the Belfort Gap.
The picture shows the first jeep to cross the
Moselle.

Below: A self-propelled gun crosses a bridge
built by the 36th Engineers at Remiremont,
France, during the establishment of the
Seventh Army's bridgehead east of the River
Moselle.

By this time, the Moselle was swollen with heavy rains and the approaches on either side were so rutted and mired that they could only be negotiated by vehicles weighing less than a quarter of a ton. Nevertheless, by September 24th the bulk of the 36th Division was safely across the river and in possession of a bridgehead extending from Remiremont to Jarmenil; this was linked with the west bank by a Bailey Bridge at Remiremont and a heavy pontoon at Jarmenil.

Meanwhile, to the north, the 45th Division was moving up to cross the river south-west of Épinal. The 157th Infantry Regiment was to cross on the left, the 180th in the centre at Épinal, and the 179th on the right. The 2nd Battalion, 36th Engineer Combat Regiment, was attached to the division with two bridge trains; one consisted of 130ft of Bailey Bridge loaded on DUKWs, five units of infantry assault bridge and eight ten-man rubber assault craft, while the other carried 240ft of treadway bridge to support heavier traffic.

The 1st Battalion of the 157th—complete with tanks, cannon and antitank guns—went across on the night of September 21st/22nd, followed by the remainder of the Regiment the next morning using a bridge built by XV Corps engineers at Châtel in the Third Army sector. After moving down the east bank, the men of the 1st Battalion had to wade back across the Moselle to reach their objective, Igney, which lay in a loop of the river. The subsequent attack, by the 3rd Battalion, was a complete success; the Germans were taken by surprise and Igney was secured after a two-hour fight. On September 23rd, to expand the bridgehead, the 1st Battalion pressed on south-eastwards up the Moselle Valley towards Hill 375 near Girmont. As they tried to clear the heavily-wooded slopes, the infantry were pinned down by intense small-arms fire and suffered severe casualties. 'B' Company stormed the hill successfully next morning, and many of the retreating Germans were killed or captured when they ran into the 3rd Battalion a short while later.

The 179th Regiment, meanwhile, had forced a passage of the Moselle at Arches in the south, although not without taking severe punishment. The enemy had blown all the bridges between Épinal and Arches, and patrols were sent out to reconnoitre possible crossing-points. During the afternoon of the 21st, supporting engineers brought up assault craft and bridging gear, while patrols on the west bank exchanged fire with small groups of enemy on the other side.

At 0400 on the 22nd, the Americans waded quietly into the water in groups of ten and climbed into their assault craft. With L Company in the lead, the little armada battled through the strong current towards the opposite bank. Suddenly, in mid-stream, mortar bombs erupted around the boats. 'L' Company went on through the spray and flying shrapnel and the leading craft reached the other side, but they met such a withering fire that they were forced to withdraw, lashed by bullets all the way. The Company suffered twenty-seven casualties. 'I' Company was more fortunate; its leading assault boat hit the far bank unopposed, and by 0615 the entire company was across, followed by the remainder of 'L' Company. After that the 179th quickly consolidated itself on the east bank and began to probe into the country beyond, although minefields, booby-traps and trees felled across roads slowed down the advance considerably.

Between the 157th and 179th Regiments, the 180th Infantry was fighting for Épinal. The enemy threw everything they had into the defence of the town; the banks of the river were heavily mined and the place was surrounded by a ring of road-blocks. Before the Americans could reach the river here, they first had to clear the considerable suburb of Épinal laying on the west bank; it was a laborious process. Tanks were used to smash some of the road-blocks, but parties detailed to clear mines, barbed wire and booby-traps met with heavy and accurate fire. By nightfall on the 21st, the 180th was effectively pinned down, and further casualties were suffered in the storm of artillery, rocket and heavy machine-gun fire directed at the regiment throughout the hours of darkness. Further progress was made at dawn, although the German rearguard fought tenaciously for every street.

At 1320, as the Americans were still battling their way towards the river, they sent back the following report to 45th Division:

"We are sending a couple of girls (FFI agents) back to your place. They have a lot of information. They report there are two bridges in town . . . the girls came over one of them. They have a map of the town that shows all the road blocks and all the mined areas. They report enemy dug in for 500 yards; this has been substantiated. We can see them and are firing on them. They report the place is heavily mined and there are considerable numbers of road-blocks all around the town. There is about half a regiment on both the east and west sides of the town, the majority in the woods on the east side."

The bridges, however, were not to stay intact for long; the German rearguard blew them both at 1600 in the wake of its withdrawal from the town. From then until dusk, while the US infantry prepared to cross the river, artillery pounded enemy transport observed leaving Épinal to the east.

The next day, September 23rd, the 180th Infantry succeeded in forcing three river crossings; all of them were bitterly contested, the men wading shoulder-deep across the river under the cover of machine-guns while

Above: Seventh Army troops march along the winding French roads at Remiremont during the expansion of their bridgehead east of the Moselle. A Sherman tank, bogged down with most of the rest of the armour by continuing wet weather, can be seen in the right background concealed behind a ruined farmhouse.

Below: Men of the 57th Signals Battalion use a captured railroad section hand car to lay field telephone lines during the exploitation of the Seventh Army's bridgehead east of the Moselle.

small-arms fire lashed the water around them. Once the first wave was across, the engineers put a ferry into operation to take more troops over and bring back the wounded. Three attempts to erect a footbridge were frustrated by the rapid current. On the night of the 23rd/24th, they did manage to establish a pair of footbridges over the debris of the blown highway bridges, and once this had been achieved the engineers really went into action. By 0500 the next morning, they had moved up a bridge train and started on the construction of a 140ft Bailey Bridge; the work was completed by 1600, in the record time of just over ten hours.

The capture of Épinal gave the Seventh Army control of one of the key centres of the Vosges, and formed an ideal base for future operations. Moreover, the town yielded supplies of all kinds, inexplicably abandoned by the Germans, as well as fifteen locomotives and many freight cars.

Over on the right flank of VI Corps, the 3rd Division was having a particularly tough time, both from the point of view of enemy opposition and the terrain it was having to fight through. The approach to the Moselle proved a far more difficult obstacle than the river itself. The enemy made full use of the thickly wooded, mountainous countryside, and at frequent intervals they had set up deep road-blocks manned by groups of thirty or forty soldiers armed with automatic and antitank weapons. Continuous rainfall had made the mountain roads absolutely impassable for armour, and every road-block consequently had to be overcome by costly infantry assaults.

At 1130 on September 20th, the 3rd Battalion of the 30th Infantry had been stopped dead in its tracks by a murderous crossfire. The men made repeated attempts to advance throughout the following day, but they were coming under fire from three sides and their progress could be measured only in yards. Groups of German infantry crawled through the undergrowth and infiltrated the American positions, attacking every half-hour or so, while significant casualties were also caused by enemy shellfire.

At 1800 on September 21st, the 7th Infantry reported: "The fighting in the woods is pretty tough. The undergrowth makes movement difficult. The Battalion has been having quite a fire fight."

The woods were particularly dense here and the Americans advanced painfully, foot by foot, crawling towards enemy positions they could not see. In the early morning, after a long, close-quarter battle, the 7th finally succeeded in reaching the Moselle opposite Rupt, and by nightfall on the 23rd they were ready to cross the river and launch an attack on the town. About midnight, a platoon of 'B' Company had a real stroke of luck when they discovered a bridge, intact amid the surrounding devastation. It was only when the infantry began to cross that they found nineteen boxes of

TNT lashed beneath the structure. These were quickly made safe, and, although the Germans subsequently made frantic efforts to recapture or destroy the bridge, they were too late to prevent the Americans from establishing a firm bridgehead on the east bank.

The 30th Infantry was the last to make the crossing in this sector. They had endured just about everthing, from torrential rain making the struggle through the dense woods a nightmare, to close-range fire at road-blocks and self-propelled artillery, 20mm flak guns and mortars. Now, at last, they had reached their objective.

So, in the last week of September, 1944, the whole of VI Corps successfully completed the crossing of the Moselle. German prisoners revealed that their original orders had been to withdraw into Germany, but these were later changed and units were ordered to hold on for twenty days until fortifications near the German border were finished.

The enemy continued to contest every foot of the American advance towards the passes through the Vosges. In the centre, the 36th Division went forward laboriously over mud-clogged secondary roads. The week's fighting had been costly for the Americans; the 142nd Infantry's 1st Battalion, for example, suffered eighty casualties while clearing the enemy from Hill 827, and many companies—weakened by severe fatigue as well as by battle casualties—were down to platoon strength.

On September 28th, the 36th Division stood 4 miles from Bruyères. Meanwhile, the 157th Infantry of the 45th Division occupied Rambervillers in the wake of a concentrated fifteen-minute barrage that stunned the defenders. Further south, the 3rd Division pushed as far uphill as Le Tholy, but not without a struggle. On September 29th, the 30th Infantry joined the 15th in readiness for an assault on this town, where German infantry with armoured support were firmly entrenched with orders to hold out to the bitter end. It was reported that these orders were to be enforced by SS troops in the rear.

At the end of September, the striking power of Patch's forces was increased by the transfer to the Seventh Army of the Third Army's XV Corps. Commanded by Major-General Wade H. Haislip, the Corps included the 2nd French Armoured Division, the 79th Infantry Division and the 106th Cavalry Troop. The 79th had just taken Luneville, north of Rambervillers; beyond lay the Forest of Parroy, which XV Corps had orders to clear in preparation for further Allied advances.

The Corps, however, was handicapped by the general supply crisis, and its stocks of ammunition and gasoline were dangerously low. It was also deficient in artillery, as was the whole of the Seventh Army and the First French Army; priority in heavy artillery had been given to the Italian campaign. The German situation, on the other hand, had improved considerably by the beginning of October. The Forest of Parroy was only a preliminary obstacle in the Americans' path; beyond it, the Germans had built continuous lines of fire-trenches and antitank ditches, as well as concrete pillboxes.

The forest itself was a confused, savage tangle of timber and undergrowth 6 miles by 5; ideal cover for its defenders, the 15th Panzer Grenadier Division. A heavy air bombardment had been scheduled to soften up the Germans prior to the Allied assault, but this was delayed because of bad weather, and when it did take place it was not sufficiently intense to hamper the enemy seriously. Nevertheless, under cover of the bombardment, the 79th Division managed to reach the edge of the forest without trouble, the 315th Infantry attacking to the north and the 313th to the south of the east-west road running through the trees.

The Germans waited until the Americans were actually in the first lanes of closely-planted trees before launching their first counter-attacks. To their astonishment the Americans saw several Mk IV tanks suddenly appear from the trees and race down the central road, blazing away at the advancing infantry with cannon and machine-guns, before darting back under cover once more.

As darkness fell on September 28th, the situation had become totally confused, with groups of enemy troops infiltrating the Allied positions and launching lightning attacks with grenades and automatic weapons, then melting away into the night. During the next forty-eight hours, the intense enemy activity brought the American advance almost to a standstill; the GIs had managed to penetrate to a depth of just 1km into the woods. During the night the Germans kept up a rapid artillery fire, and the Americans were forced to cover their foxholes with logs and branches for protection against the shrapnel that scythed through the treetops. The enemy kept their main forces well behind their nebulous front, sending only small groups forward to attack when the US infantry could be heard moving forward through the undergrowth.

On October 1st, the 314th Regiment was ordered to cut off the southern salient of the woods and push through the 313th's lines to join the 315th north of the central road. Their advance initially went well, but then it was checked by a strong infantry counter-attack supported by six tanks. However, continual American pressure in the centre forced the Germans to reinforce their lines here with troops drawn from the north and south sectors, and its was not long before the 314th was able to forge ahead once more. Nevertheless, the advance was still a foot-by-foot affair and by October 8th, the wood was still only half cleared.

A 4.2 mortar battalion lays down a barrage at
Le Tholy, France, during the Seventh Army's
assault on the Vosges in October 1944.

A new assault and cover plan were launched simultaneously at 0630 the following day. As a diversionary measure, tanks brought up by the 1st Battalion of the 313th Regiment opened fire from positions south of the forest; the Germans rose to the bait and returned the fire throughout the morning. While the tanks and artillery slogged away at each other, the 2nd Battalion of the 315th pushed towards the high ground at the eastern edge of the forest, and from the south the 2nd Battalion of the 314th—with armoured support—moved down the track of an abandoned narrow-gauge railway in a manoeuvre designed to outflank the main enemy strongpoint deep in the forest.

By mid-afternoon, all the American units were in position and the final attack was launched under cover of a smokescreen. The 2,000 German troops detailed to stop the Allied advance through the forest at all costs fought tenaciously, but they were almost completely enveloped now and by midnight it was all over. The surviving Germans abandoned their last defensive positions and slipped away under cover of darkness, leaving their casualties scattered among the wreckage of knocked-out tanks and shattered bunkers.

The week-long battle for the Forest of Parroy had been characterised by the bold use of armour, particularly by the Germans. The density of the trees had generally forced the Panzers to keep to the trails and fire-breaks, but wherever a clearing or thin growth made it possible they had struck away from the roads. They had also played a major part in keeping the German defences supplied when trucks had been unable to operate on the sodden trails.

During the early days of October, the weather stayed firmly on the side of the Germans. The heavy rainfall had turned the ground at the foot of the Vosges into swamp land, and the American armour spearheading the Seventh Army's renewed drive towards the high ground beyond the Forest of Parroy quickly became bogged down. This, together with the holding action in the woods, gave the Germans vital extra days in which to reorganise themselves and strengthen their main defensive line, which ran from the swamps to the High Vosges and which was now 2-3 miles deep. To the enemy rear, massive rail and road movements of troops and equipment went on unhindered beneath the blanket of rain and fog which kept the Allied tactical air forces on the ground.

In mid-October, the 44th Infantry Division joined the Seventh Army, relieving the 79th Division, which had been in action continuously for more than four months. The 44th had its baptism of fire on October 25th, when local fighting broke out in various sectors of XV Corps front.

Meanwhile, to the south, VI Corps continued to move forward

laboriously. The biggest single success was achieved by the 3rd and 36th Divisions, which launched an attack under cover of a clever piece of deception. For four days, beginning on October 15th, every possible step was taken to make the enemy believe that the American assault was to develop from a point west of Le Tholy; in fact, it was to be launched further to the north. The 3rd Division radio nets continued to operate around Le Tholy, dummy artillery emplacement were built in the area and an increasing number of combat patrols were pushed out. The 36th Division also stepped up patrol activity along the southern portion of its line. On the right flank of the front, the VI Corps Piper Cub spotter aircraft flew frequent sorties as though pinpointing enemy gun positions and dumps preparatory to a big artillery bombardment. The deception was to continue even after H-Hour, when a dummy armoured group radio net was to be opened to foster the impression that a tank attack was under way from Le Tholy.

Meanwhile, the 3rd Division moved under cover of darkness to its jump-off position south of Rambervillers, carefully camouflaging dumps, command installations and gun positions. Guns were moved singly into their new emplacements over a period of days, and reconnaissance parties wore the insignia of the 45th Division. Finally, on October 20th, everything was ready. At dawn, under cover of a heavy barrage, the 3rd Division launched a powerful punch at the German lines and captured several key terrain features. The enemy reacted with determined counter-attacks in a bid to dislodge the Americans; on October 26th and 27th, the 30th Infantry Regiment was subjected to the most concentrated artillery bombardment experienced by any Seventh Army unit since the landings in southern France, but the infantry managed to hold on. By the end of the month they had broken through the rough mountain terrain to seize the high ground dominating the Meurthe River Valley in the St Die area, taking over 5,000 prisoners in the process.

While this attack was in progress, the 36th Division had run into trouble. At 0845 on October 23rd, General Dahlquist directed the 141st Infantry to send out a force of company or battalion strength to work along a forest trail east of Bruyères and secure certain high ground. The mission was assigned to the 1st Battalion, 141st Regiment. The men moved off into the forest, and it was not long before things started to go wrong; first of all, contact was lost with the rest of the Regiment—and then the Germans attacked in strength, overrunning the command post and driving back the Headquarters and Battalion staffs. Within half an hour the Battalion was completely surrounded.

On October 25th, the 2nd Battalion, 141st Infantry, tried to force a supply route through to the trapped men, but could get no nearer than 1,200 yards. The Germans were covering the trail with machine-guns and artillery, and one of their observation posts in the forest directed accurate fire on to every vehicle that tried to run the gauntlet.

The plight of the surrounded combat elements of the 1st Battalion—some 240 men under the command of First Lieutenant Martin J. Higgins, Jr—was now critical; the Germans kept infiltrating their positions, about a mile north of La Houssiere, and desperate hand-to-hand fighting continued. It was only a question of time before the Americans, short of ammunition as they were, would be compelled to surrender.

That same day, the 442nd Infantry (Nisei) Regiment was detailed to batter a road through the German ring and rescue the stranded battalion. If any unit could do the job, it was this one. The Nisei was composed almost entirely of Japanese-Americans—hardy fighters who had already been in action for a week without respite.

Meanwhile, attempts were being made to supply the Battalion by air. The first drop, made by four C-47s at 1100 on October 27th, was a total failure because of bad weather; one of the transport aircraft crashed in the mountains, killing its crew. Over the next two days, however, other aircraft managed to drop rations, ammunition, plasma and radio batteries with some success, although a dense ground fog made it hard for the crews to pick out details and some of their cargoes inevitably fell into enemy hands. Tragically, one of the C-47s was shot down by friendly antiaircraft fire as it crossed the front line. The 131st Field Artillery Battalion also tried to fire supplies to the surrounded men; shells normally used for propaganda leaflets were filled with medical supplies and bars of chocolate and lobbed into the woods by 105mm and 155mm howitzers. Unfortunately, most of them buried themselves deeply in the muddy ground and were lost.

At 1030 on October 26th, the commanders of VI Corps and the 36th Division arrived at the 141st Regimental Command Post to survey the situation. Soon afterwards, the Divisional Commander ordered the Regimental Commander to have the 1st Battalion attack immediately to the west in an attempt to break out of the encirclement while ammunition lasted. These orders were duly passed on by radio, and at 1312 a message was received from the Battalion to the effect that contact had been made with the enemy at three points. The following day, another radio report stated that the morale of the men was high, although their physical state was fairly low. The attempt to break out of the trap had cost the battalion four men killed, twenty-eight wounded and forty-three missing.

By this time, the men of the Nisei were near, and on the afternoon of October 29th the Divisional Commander sent a signal to the encircled men

Men of the Japanese-American 442nd
Infantry (Nisei) Regiment survey the Bruyère
sector in the Vosges from a copse torn by
artillery and mortar fire. This Regiment of the
Seventh Army's 36th Division took part in
fierce fighting to relieve a surrounded
battalion on the ridge (seen in the background
of the picture) a few days later.

saying that the 442nd was thrusting through to within 700 yards of them, and ordering patrols to be sent out to contact the Japanese-Americans. Lieutenant Higgins replied that he simply did not have enough men to spare for such a venture; the Germans were very active and an attack was thought to be imminent.

The advance of the 442nd was agonisingly slow. There were minefields and road-blocks all along the route; the Nisei attacked each of the latter with bayonets and grenades, displaying all the suicidal courage of their adopted country's enemies in the Pacific. The Germans suffered heavy casualties. Little quarter was given. As each road-block was cleared by the Nisei, it was shovelled aside by a tankdozer to clear the way for supporting American armour.

On October 30th, a heavy artillery and mortar barrage was laid down on the ridge separating the 442nd from the 1st Battalion, and at 0900 both forces attacked. At 1600 the long-awaited radio message crackled over the air to the command post: "Patrol from the 442nd here. Tell them we love them."

The isolated Battalion had been reached by patrols of the Nisei's 3rd Battalion. They dug in around Higgins' battered GIs, and the 442nd's 100th Battalion moved up on the right. This valiant relief action had brought the Japanese-American Regiment's total casualties for the October fighting to 117 men killed, 657 wounded and 40 missing.

As November opened, VI Corps was faced with three main problems. The first was to bring the left and right flanks of the Corps up to the salient held by the 3rd Division along the Meurthe; the second, to introduce the newly arrived 100th and 103rd Infantry Divisions to combat as painlessly as possible; and the third, to regroup the entire Corps to attack across the Meurthe, crack the German winter line, penetrate the Vosges passes and drive on beyond to the Rhine. The two new divisions had arrived from the United States together with the 14th Armoured Division, and were in action within a month of landing at Marseilles.

During its first week of combat, the 103rd Division came face to face with the new German 'scorched earth' policy. On November 8th, Gestapo HQ at St Die received orders from General Heckel to form arson and demolition squads for the purpose of destroying all towns in the wake of the German withdrawal. The Gestapo wasted no time. Within forty-eight hours, its commandos had begun an organised programme of burning, looting and mass destruction. On November 11th, all women, children and old people were evacuated from the portion of St Die that lay north of the Meurthe River under the pretext that the US Air Force was about to launch a massive raid on the town with fire bombs; all able-bodied men had previously been sent to Strasbourg.

Throughout the following night and day, the evacuated part of St Die was systematically looted by German soldiers. Then, at noon on November 13th, the work of destruction began, the demolition squads using gasoline and incendiary bombs to ignite the fires and small charges of dynamite to destroy machinery in local plants.

On the night of November 17th/18th, a patrol of the 410th Infantry entered what was left of St Die. Only the town clock still stood intact, rising like an accusing finger from a sea of ruins. And St Die was not the only town to suffer; further south Corcieux, St Leonard, Ste Marguerite and Gerardmer were also put to the torch, although a rapid Allied advance in the Gerardmer sector prevented total destruction here.

While the five towns burned, the Germans launched a series of fanatical counter-attacks, and the Americans once again found themselves involved in savage fighting. The 142nd Infantry's experiences during this phase were typical. The regiment's mission was to drive down a narrow valley to reach the Meurthe. For tactical reasons all open ground had to be avoided, and the Americans moved slowly up and down ridges under cover of woods, often fighting their way literally from tree to tree. Enemy artillery had a devastating effect, the shells bursting among the treetops and peppering the area with wicked slivers of wood as well as shrapnel. The weather, too, added to the infantry's misery; heavy rain turned to fog and wet, clinging snow. Between November 4th and 12th, the regiment lost 44 men killed, 235 wounded and 7 missing—added to which there were 345 non-combat casualties, mostly due to exposure and 'trench foot'.

It was all uphill work, and to make matters worse the Allied supply system still appeared to be chaotic. The ammunition situation was critical; the 131st Field Artillery Battalion, for example, could have fired off ten days' supply in as many minutes—a fact that annoyed gunners who remembered Cassino, where 6,000 shells had been hurled against the enemy in a single day.

Despite all the difficulties, by November 19th, four American divisions faced the Meurthe River defences on VI Corps front, ready for the push against the next major objective: Strasbourg. A simultaneous thrust was to be launched against Saverne by XV Corps, while the First French Army was to burst through the Belfort Gap.

Facing the Allies were 13,000 German troops, with orders to fight to the last man. Whether those orders would be obeyed, the French and Americans had no way of knowing—but every man was grimly aware that the sternest test was yet to come.

Above: '... heavy rain turned to fog and wet, clinging snow'. Despite this and the wooded, hilly terrain, men of the 142nd Infantry Regiment, 36th Division, seen here near Langefosse, forced their way down to the Meurthe River against heavy German counter-attacks during the Seventh Army's thrust towards Strasbourg in November, 1944.

Below: French soldiers of the 155th Field Artillery Battery clear snow away from their position in preparation for the Seventh Army's drive against Strasbourg.

Above: Loading a 105mm howitzer during the preparatory softening up of the German positions at St Die, France, during the Seventh Army's offensive against the Saverne Gap and Strasbourg.

Below: Infantrymen take a lift up to the front on tanks during preparations for an attack on Struth, France, during the final stages of the Seventh Army's assault on the High Vosges in November, 1944.

VIII

The Seventh Army's mission in the offensive of November, 1944, appeared simple enough on paper; to destroy the enemy forces in the zone west of the Rhine, capture Strasbourg and maintain contact with the right flank of Twelfth Army Group. VI Corps was to launch its assault not later than D-plus-2 on the axis St Die-Strasbourg; XV Corps was to strike on D-Day itself, secure Sarrebourg, force the Saverne Gap and stand ready to exploit its passage east of the Vosges. After this initial phase was completed, it was planned to pull the 45th Division out of the line for a time.

The attack opened at 0700 on November 13th, with the 44th Division pushing eastwards to Sarrebourg and the 79th Division on the southern flank opening the way for the French 2nd Armoured Division, which was to spearhead the drive through the Saverne Gap to Strasbourg. The initial Allied thrust was met by strong enemy rearguard action supported by heavy artillery and mortar fire, but as the 44th Division gained momentum the German defences in the foothills of the Vosges began to crumble and it was not long before the enemy was in retreat along the whole XV Corps front.

Meanwhile, the French had been making good progress in their drive through the Saverne Gap, following up the 79th Division's punch. At 1400 on November 21st, a French armoured task force rumbled on to the Alsace Plain south of the Saverne. The Allies were now in possession of a route through the Vosges, albeit a minor and tenuous one, but with the capture of Pfalsbourg on the 23rd, following a flanking movement by the 79th Division, the Franco-American force obtained a firm foothold on the eastern side of the mountains. Ahead of them now lay Strasbourg; beyond lay the broad ribbon of the Rhine and, rising dimly from the far horizon, the Black Forest.

Strasbourg is the metropolis of the Alsace Plain. As well as main road and rail communications, natural and artificial waterways also contribute to its strategic importance. The Rhine-Rhône and Marne-Rhine Canals both end at Strasbourg, joining the city by water with southern and northern France. But Strasbourg—as the political capital of Alsace, a province annexed by Germany in 1871 and returned to France in 1918, only to be re-occupied by the Nazis in 1940—was also of immense psychological value to the Allies; its liberation was vital to the prestige of France.

At 1130 on November 22nd, General Leclerc received orders to take his 2nd Armoured Division to the aid of VI Corps in the projected assault on Strasbourg—or, if circumstances were favourable, to attack the city alone. The attack called for a quick, concerted movement on the city from all possible directions, with lightning probes against the defences. These included sixteen forts, located on the main roads into Strasbourg or on elevated points outside. The 2nd Armoured was given the task of breaking through the weakest point in the defensive wall and driving on to the Rhine.

The Allied columns approached Strasbourg from the north, west and south-west, with the 2nd Armoured in the centre. The 2nd Armoured's spearhead, known as Task Force Rouvillois, followed the Marne-Rhine Canal eastward from Saverne and then struck south towards the northern suburbs of Strasbourg, probing for a weak link in the enemy defences. At 1030, just over three hours after the Task Force set out on its mission, the command post of the 2nd Armoured Division picked up a cryptic, coded message from its commander: "Tissue est dans Iode—Cloth is in Iodine." This meant, simply, that the Task Force had battered its way into Strasbourg and was now driving on towards the Kehl bridge, a key crossing-point over the Rhine.

Meanwhile, VI Corps had reached the Meurthe River and was preparing to cross it and drive for the Vosges passes in the south. The task of establishing a bridgehead on the east bank was assigned to the 3rd Division, supported by direct fire from tanks and tank destroyers. H-Hour was scheduled for 0645 on November 20th. A last-minute reconnaissance revealed that the river was in flood, with its banks probably too soft to support armour.

At 0545, the American artillery opened up with a thunderous barrage; the 3rd Division's guns alone fired over 6,500 rounds in sixty minutes. While the bombardment was in progress, elements of the 7th and 30th Infantry slipped across the river in rubber assault craft while it was still dark and established themselves on the opposite bank. The bulk of the 3rd Division made the crossing at dawn, under cover of a heavy smokescreen laid down by the 3rd Chemical Battalion. The 30th Infantry turned north along the Meurthe to consolidate the crossing, while the 7th Infantry overran La Voivre. This little town had been heavily mined and booby-trapped by the Germans before they pulled out, and in clearing it the Americans suffered 150 casualties.

As the vanguard of the 3rd Division entered Alsace, the Americans had a grim reminder of what they were fighting against. Divisional G-2 had received reports of a concentration camp at Natzviller, 8 miles from Rothau, and on November 26th, a reconnaissance team went out to investigate. They found all the paraphernalia of horror; electrified barbed-wire fences, 'shower rooms' where victims were murdered, and a crematorium. The camp had a normal capacity of 3,000 prisoners and a maximum of 4,200; the vast majority were political opponents of the Nazis, but the Americans also found bible students, priests of various denominations, homosexuals, 'socially unfit' elements, habitual criminals—and, of course, Jews. Most of the prisoners had been evacuated by the Germans on November 16th; plans had been made to destroy the place and remove all documents, but the American advance had been so swift that the SS demolition teams had not had time to carry out their work.

Although enemy resistance in the 3rd Division sector was rapidly collapsing, some German strongpoints offered fanatical resistance. One was an old Maginot Line fortress north of Mutzig, and 'E' Company of the 30th Infantry was given the job of neutralising it. Despite close-range fire from 155mm howitzers, the enemy garrison refused to surrender, sending out a continual stream of signals requesting ammunition, food and medical supplies.

On December 2nd, the XII Tactical Air Command bombed the fort, but with no apparent effect on either the structure or its occupants. Two days later it was the infantry's turn. Under cover of brisk machine-gun and mortar fire a team of volunteers charged the fortress in a captured German half-track crammed with 3½ tons of TNT. They got the vehicle across the surrounding ditch and up against the wall under cover of darkness, then set the fuzes and dived for cover. A few seconds later, a mighty explosion blew the half-track to pieces and blasted part of the wall into rubble. Soon afterwards, a small group of the enemy tried to escape through the hole. After a brief exchange of small-arms fire, two officers and seven men were captured, the remainder having either retreated into the fort or been killed. From their prisoners the American learned that eighty-two German soldiers were still inside the fort, but after a second air strike on December 5th, they too came out into the open and surrendered.

The Allied advance went on all along the Vosges Front. On November 22nd, a company of the 409th Infantry liberated the eastern part of St Die;

later, the Mayor expressed the gratitude of the citizens by renaming the town's main square in honour of its liberators, the 103rd Division. The Americans also captured Barr and Selestat, although not without first overcoming stiff resistance. The cryptic phraseology of the Seventh Army Intelligence Summary for this period tells its own story:

"Four battalions were involved in the attack on Selestat. Two battalions of the 409th Infantry were already fighting in the northern part of the city; the 2nd Battalion of the 143rd advanced directly east from Chatenois; while the 3rd Battalion of the 142nd moved on Selestat from the south. On December 2nd, the 2nd Battalion of the 143rd engaged the enemy in a heavy fire fight in the city and encountered machine-gun and small-arms fire, booby-traps, mines and trip-wires. An enemy command post was taken and three German staff officers captured. The 3rd Battalion of the 142nd Infantry, having crossed to the east of the Colmar highway, moved out to attack the south-eastern sector of Selestat at 0630 on December 2nd. The advance was made against intense sniper fire. At 1600, an enemy column of 150 men moving toward Selestat from the south-east was dispersed by artillery fire.

"On December 2nd, Company K led the 3rd Battalion in clearing the south-east corner of the town and reached a bridge over the Ill River which the Germans had blown. Heavy fire stopped the advance. On the next day, Company E of the 409th Infantry reached the river and fanned to the south to make contact with the 3rd Battalion of the 142nd Regiment. By 1645 on December 4th, the city was completely occupied."

The relative ease of VI Corps's penetration of the High Vosges—a natural obstacle considered to be impregnable through centuries of military history—came as a shock to the Germans. On November 21st, General Thumm, commanding the German LXIV Corps opposing VI Corps's advance, issued an order of the day in which he exhorted his soldiers to fight "standing at the borders of our fatherland" for the life of the people, of the soldiers's families, and of Germany herself. "The order to hold out to the last man must be executed under all circumstances . . . Great decisions are being made here and now. I expect all commanders, leaders and troops to hold out, not to lose their nerve, and fight to the last breath . . . The decision falls on this side of the Rhine."

Although by the end of December the enemy's Vosges line had been breached and Allied troops had already reached the Rhine at Mulhouse and Strasbourg, the Germans showed no sign of ordering a general withdrawal from the area between these two cities, the Colmar Pocket. In fact, it appeared that they had every intention of making its capture as costly as possible for the Allies, even if it meant sacrificing their own chances of survival.

The Seventh Army, in accordance with the original plan, was to have attempted a crossing of the Rhine north of Strasbourg in December, but the presence of a large German force in the Colmar Pocket caused Eisenhower to change both the mission of the Seventh Army and its direction of advance. The new strategy called for a swing north astride the Vosges in an advance co-ordinated with the Third Army; its object was to breach the famous Siegfried Line between Lauterbourg on the Rhine and Saarbrücken, destroying the German forces still west of the Rhine in the process.

Moving an entire army front is a highly complicated manoeuvre at the best of times; the Seventh Army had to carry it out while still engaging the enemy in some sectors. Nevertheless, the task was accomplished by the end of November, and on December 5th both XV and VI Corps stood ready to launch their new drive to the north. XV Corps now comprised the 44th and 100th Infantry Divisions, with the newly attached 12th Armoured Division. In the VI Corps sector, the 45th and 79th Divisions were still in the line, with the 14th Armoured and 103rd Infantry Divisions assembled to the rear in readiness for a general offensive. The 32nd Infantry Division continued to hold Strasbourg and its environs, while the 36th Division and the French 2nd Armoured Division remained in the line from Selestat to the Rhine.

In the fighting between November 15th and 30th, the German forces facing the Seventh Army had lost some 17,500 men, 13,000 of them taken prisoner; they now had only 14,000 men against seven Allied divisions. The Seventh Army's abrupt switch to a northerly advance, however—as well as robbing the Allies of the chance of taking a short cut into the heart of Germany—gave the enemy additional time in which to strengthen their West Wall defences along the Rhine. The weather, too, continued to be of advantage to the Germans; December in Alsace is a cloudy month, with ground fog and drizzle, and only on five days did the murk clear sufficiently to allow the Tactical Air Force to give close support to the Seventh Army.

Allied Intelligence had already predicted that the Germans would make a stand either at the Maginot or Siegfried Lines, but aerial photographs showed few signs of activity in the Maginot Line area—except for some scattered digging in the mountains and around Bitche—so it appeared that the Germans intended to fight only a delaying action in this area while they fell back on the Siegfried Line.

Seventh Army's plan for the advance on the Siegfried Line envisaged a six-pronged drive, with XV Corps on the left and VI Corps on the right. The divisions involved were—from west to east—the 44th, 100th, 45th, 103rd, 14th Armoured and 79th.

On December 3rd, Major-General Robet T. Frederick, who had commanded the Airborne Task Force in southern France, assumed command of 45th Division in place of General Eagles, who was wounded when his jeep ran over a mine. Frederick arrived just in time to witness some tough fighting as the Division struck towards Lembach on December 5th. The town fell on the 14th to units of the 180th Infantry, and two days later elements of the 45th Division crossed the German border and made contact with the Siegfried Line defences.

Further south, the 79th Division had started its drive against Gambsheim and Haguenau on December 7th; this developed into a dramatic race along the west bank of the Rhine to Lauterbourg, the Division's armour battering its way through stiff opposition until it reached the Lauter River. Then, suddenly, the enemy melted away; here, too, they had pulled back behind the Siegfried Line, enabling the 79th Division to cross the Lauter without hindrance.

Between the 45th and 79th Divisions, the 103rd moved on Wissembourg. Heavy rains had swollen the Zintel River in places to a width of nearly a quarter of a mile and all the bridges were out, but the 410th Infantry managed to cross the torrent over improvised footbridges to occupy Mertzwiller. From there the 103rd pushed on through the deserted Maginot Line, meeting no enemy opposition until they reached the town of Climbach on December 14th. Here, strong German defences brought the Americans to a standstill.

The task of planning the attack on the town was assigned to Lieutenant-Colonel John P. Blackshear, executive officer of the 411th Infantry. The main object was to sever the lines of communication between Climbach and Lembach, the target of the 45th Division.

Task Force Blackshear moved up the road on the morning of December 14th in a long motorised column. Suddenly, as the leading tank destroyers crossed the ridge and headed down into the valley where Climbach nestled, the Germans opened up with a furious artillery barrage. One of the armoured vehicles slewed off the road, burning fiercely; the other four spread out and returned the fire, but three of them were quickly knocked out. While this artillery duel was in progress, however, riflemen and machine-gunners managed to secure the two hills flanking Climbach, and an attack was mounted on the town under cover of a bombardment by the 411th's artillery battalion. By 1800, Climbach was in Allied hands; the Germans counter-attacked soon afterwards with four tanks and 200 men, but they were beaten off after the 2nd and 3rd Battalions of the 410th Infantry had gone to the 411th's aid.

The 45th and 103rd Divisions both crossed the German border on the same day, December 16th. The 103rd advanced up to the Siegfried Line; the 409th Infantry took Rott and the 410th ran into heavy fire from the line itself. The 411th—after overcoming resistance north of Climbach—reached the centre of the Siegfried Line defences on December 17th. All three regiments were supported by mule trains because the ground was impassable for motorised transport. The 14th Armoured Division had also moved up by this time, so that by mid-December all four divisions on VI Corps were in the line and poised for the assault on Germany's West Wall.

On the left flank of the Seventh Army, XV Corps with two infantry divisions had initially outdistanced VI Corps in the dash across the Alsace Plain before grinding to a standstill at Bitche, a key German stronghold. All along the western front the Germans had made little use of the Maginot Line forts. The reason was simple—they were facing in the wrong direction, having been built to fire east and north. The four large forts guarding the line between Bitche and Holbach, however, were so situated that they commanded an excellent field of fire to the south. They were also linked together by a series of long block houses. The Germans had been unable to crack these formidable defensive positions in 1940; the forts had, in fact, held out until after the armistice.

This tough nut had to be cracked before the Allied advance could continue, and on December 13th the two strongest—Schiesseck and Simershof—were attacked by the 100th and 44th Divisions respectively. Eight of Fort Simershof's pillboxes were sited on a hilltop south-east of Holbach. A thousand yards further south were the personnel and ammunition entrances to the fort, and it was from this point that elaborate underground communications, lighting and ventilation systems were controlled.

The 71st Infantry Regiment, which was to spearhead the attack on Simershof, planned to outflank the fort on the eastern side, destroy the personnel and ammunition entraces and then carry out an assault in the wake of an intense air and artillery bombardment. It was soon apparent, however, that the operation was going to be a costly one for both sides. The 1st and 3rd Battalions of the 71st went in on schedule, only to be hurled back by an insupportable fire. On the second attempt they stormed the pillboxes covering the gap between Schiesseck and Simershof, suffering heavy casualties, and pushed on to outflank the latter fort as planned. For four days, the Germans made repeated attempts to dislodge them, but the Americans hung on grimly and waited for the main assault.

Above: Troops newly arrived from the
United States assemble with their tank
destroyer vehicles in Sarrebourg for the
Seventh Army's Christmas offensive against
the Siegfried Line in 1944.

Below: Part of the wreckage of Fort
Simershof, a Maginot Line strongpoint,
defended for five days by the Germans against
intense air and artillery bombardment and
repeated assaults by the Seventh Army during
their Christmas offensive.

On December 17th, after being held up by the continual bad weather, Marauders of the XII Tactical Air Force flew three bombing missions against Simershof. This was followed, the next day, by a concentrated artillery barrage laid down by the 156th and 242nd Field Artillery Battalions. When the smoke cleared, three enemy pillboxes had been so severely battered that they had to be abandoned, a fourth had its concrete roof—10ft thick—blasted in by a direct hit from a 240mm howitzer shell, and several less well protected gun positions were reduced to rubble.

Meanwhile, beginning on December 14th, the 2nd Battalion of the 71st Infantry and 'C' Company of the 63rd Engineer Battalion had been working hard at dealing with the personnel and ammunition entrances on the southern hill. The ammunition entrance was smoked and sealed off within a few hours, and on December 15th the engineers—covered by heavy fire from riflemen, tanks and tank destroyers—cut a path through the two barbed-wire entanglements ringing the personnel entrance, blew holes in the turrets with satchel charges and dropped a bangalore torpedo down one of the holes to destroy the diesel power plant.

Over the next two days, more charges of TNT and phosphorous grenades were dropped into the labyrinth of subterranean tunnels through holes blasted by the armour-piercing shells of the tank destroyers. By the evening of December 17th, after the air and ground bombardment, the Americans had forced their way into the underground perimeter of the fort, pushing on into its recesses down twenty-three flights of stairs. At the bottom, a narrow-gauge railway vanished into a tunnel which seemed to lead to the heart of the fortress. The GIs prepared to move along it, but the Germans resisted fiercely. After several hours of this unreal, troglodytic warfare in the shadowy passageways, the Americans decided that the easiest method of dealing with the enemy was to blow up the stairway and destroy the ventilation system. Six hundred pounds of TNT turned the stairway into a pile of twisted metal, and tankdozers shovelled tons of earth over the ventilation shafts. Before long, the Germans inside were collapsing like flies from the effect of the suffocating, blinding gases of their own heavy guns, and when the lights failed further resistance became impossible. On December 18th, the garrison of Fort Simershof surrendered.

Fort Schiesseck, however—or at least part of it—continued to hold out in the face of repeated assaults by the 100th Division. Supported by the fire of two other, smaller forts, it stood astride a large barren hill commanding the north-western approaches to Bitche. Nine of its eleven pillboxes were on top of the hill; the others were at its base. All were built of reinforced concrete and steel, extended three or four stories deep underground and were inter-connected. Each was surrounded by a moat and was equipped with tubes down which grenades could be rolled against attackers. Three of them had retractable turrets and all were heavily armed. Moreover, any force attacking the fort first had to cross several hundred yards of open ground commanded by the enemy artillery.

A probing attack by the 1st Battalion, 398th Infantry, on December 14th soon became pinned down, and the 100th Division planned a major attack on the fort. The main effort was to be made by the 398th Regiment on the left, while the 397th on the right was to hold its ground and stand ready to carry out a diversionary attack. The 3rd Battalion of the 398th was to lead the assault, with two companies sharing the task of knocking out the pillboxes. One platoon was assigned to each pillbox; while two squads provided covering fire, the third would go in and button up the apertures, paving the way for the engineers and tankdozers to get on with the real demolition work. The whole operation was to be supported by chemical mortars, 81mm mortars and tanks.

On December 15th and 16th, the target was softened up by heavy artillery fire and the faithful XII TAF. Twenty-seven tons of bombs fell in the target area and made 32 direct hits, while the artillery fired off 481 rounds and reported 117 direct hits. The weight of explosive, however, had little effect. Forward observers were staggered to see 240mm shells ricochet off the 4ft-thick walls of the casemate. Even on the second day, when some of the guns were moved up to the crest of the hill and opened fire at point-blank range, there was still no decisive result. The Germans simply retracted everything and went underground to wait for the barrage to lift.

The attack proper opened on the morning of December 17th under cover of diversionary activity by the 397th Infantry. After a ninety-minute air and artillery bombardment, the 398th's two assaulting companies moved forward under a light rolling barrage which lifted as they came up to their objectives.

Company L and I assault platoons quickly knocked out blocks 9 and 10, according to plan, but block 11 proved a tougher proposition; it was the personnel entrance, and was more heavily defended than its companions. Three riflemen rushed the block and dropped grenades into its turret to silence the heavy machine-gun, but then enemy mortars opened up, killing three men and driving the rest back. An engineer braved a storm of small-arms fire to dash across and place a satchel charge against the pillbox's armoured door; he got safely under cover again, but the charge failed to explode. A bazooka team then tried to get into position to fire on the door, but both men were killed by a mortar bomb. A second team was more fortunate; one of their rockets hit the satchel charge, which went off with a violent explosion and blew the door clean out. The infantry charged the entrance as soon as the smoke cleared and got inside without difficulty, only to find their way barred by a sealed inner door. This too was blown by the engineers, who also wrecked the staircase leading into the depths. Then the troops withdrew and a tankdozer came up to cover the block with earth.

After capturing the first four blocks, Companies I and L dug in while XII TAF hammered Fort Otterbiel, artillery from which had caused many American casualties during the assault on Schiesseck. That night 100th Division artillery blasted aside the barbed-wire entanglements that surrounded the remaining blocks, and on December 18th the infantry renewed the attack. The last of Fort Schiesseck's blockhouses finally surrendered on the 20th, its garrison having held out for forty-eight hours in the teeth of point-blank artillery fire and repeated infantry assaults.

So, after a week of hard fighting, the 100th Division was now free to clear Bitche and advance northwards to the 44th Division flank for the drive on the Siegfried Line. Meanwhile, as XV Corps breached the Maginot Line, VI Corps was cautiously probing the Siegfried Line's defences. The Germans withdrew warily as the Americans advanced into the defensive zone, preferring to oppose them with tanks and self-propelled guns rather than give away the location of their main artillery defences. Nevertheless, Seventh Army G-2 had been able to pinpoint the strongpoints as early as December 7th, and preparations were already under way for a series of frontal assaults on the weak sectors.

Then, suddenly, there came yet another change in strategy. The Seventh Army was ordered to discontinue its northerly drive and prepare a defensive line. The 100th Division went back to the positions it had occupied before the attack on Forst Schiesseck; the 180th Infantry, 45th Division, pulled back to the south of the Lauter River and the other divisions dug in where they were.

To the north, in the Ardennes, the last German offensive of the war had begun on December 16th, with seventeen divisions hammering a wedge 35 miles deep and 60 miles wide into the Allied lines in Belgium and Luxembourg in what was later to be called the Battle of the Bulge. There followed ten days of feverish activity as the Allies readjusted their lines to counter the new threat. On December 19th, the Third Army's XII Corps took over the III Corps's front, enabling the latter to move north for an attack on the southern flank of von Rundstedt's Ardennes salient. To compensate for this northerly shift, the Seventh Army extended its left boundary to St Avold and prepared defences on a front stretching 84 miles westward from the Rhine. The move took four days and was completed on December 26th. During this period elements of the 42nd, 63rd and 70th

Divisions joined the Seventh Army fresh from the United States; these units had not yet completed their combat training and it would be some time before they could be used in the line.

Although the drive into Germany had been brought temporarily to a standstill, Seventh Army Intelligence used the delay to good advantage in amassing further information about the German defences across the Rhine. Rail movements, prisoner-of-war reports and photo interpretation indicated a build-up of enemy forces in the Saarbrücken area as well as in the Colmar Pocket and east of the Rhine Valley. On December 24th, Seventh Army received this warning from Sixth Army Group: "Excellent agent sources report enemy units building up in the Black Forest area for offensive. Other indications for imminent enemy aggressive action exist. Imperative that all defensive precautions be immediately effective."

As the picture of the enemy's intentions became clearer, the Seventh Army's sense of anti-climax gave way to one of danger. A Sixth Army Group order of December 21st had directed the Seventh to yield ground rather than endanger the integrity of its forces, and an alternative main line of resistance was prepared in the Maginot Line. This was finished on December 30th, and that same day another radio message from Sixth Army Group warned that: "A hostile attack against your flank west of Bitche may force you to give ground from your main position. To meet such a possibility, it is necessary that your west flank be protected by a reserve battle position. With this in mind, reconnaissance and organisation of a reserve battle position will be instituted without delay along high ground on the general lines: Hill east of Landroff—Benestroff—Sarre Union—Ingwiller. One half of each division and attached troops currently earmarked as SHAEF reserve, located in your area, may be employed at any given period of time to assist in organisation of ground, provided troops so employed can be reassembled and prepared for movement on eight hour notice. . ."

On New Year's Eve, General Patch visited the XV Corps Command Post at Fénétrange to confer with the Commanding Generals of VI and XV Corps. He came straight to the point. A massive enemy attack could be expected in the early hours of New Year's Day.

IX

As Sixth Army Group had predicted, the Germans struck hard in the closing hours of the old year. Enemy documents captured later revealed that their High Command West had concluded from the Allied withdrawal of bridgeheads in the Sarre area that the forces opposing them on this front south from the Ardennes to the Rhine had been seriously weakened. On December 21st, the German Army Group G had, therefore, been directed to exploit the situation, mounting local attacks in readiness for a general offensive aimed at regaining the Saverne Gap. Operation 'Nordwind' was the offensive's codename; the Führer himself had ordered it to start at 2300 on December 31st, 1944.

At that time the Seventh Army occupied an 84-mile front from the Rhine to a point a few miles west of Saarbrücken, and a flank along the Rhine north and south of Strasbourg. VI Corps held the right from the Rhine to Bitche with the 79th and 45th Infantry in the line and the 14th Armoured Division in reserve. On the left flank of VI Corps, holding a front of some 10 miles in the Low Vosges, was Task Force Hudelson.

To the left of this force, XV Corps maintained a line running westwards to within a few miles of Saarbrücken, employing the 100th, 44th and 103rd Infantry Divisions with the 106th Cavalry Group on their left. Most of the Rhine flank, stretching some 40 miles, was the responsibility of Task Force Herren and Task Force Linden, composed of infantry elements of the 70th and 42nd Divisions respectively.

It was the 44th Infantry, deployed between Sarreguemines and Rimling, which took the full impetus of the enemy's right flank drive. Within a few hours, the whole divisional front was engaged. On the left, between Sarreguemines and Folsperviller, the 114th Infantry Regiment—with strong artillery support—shattered an enemy attempt to exploit their Blies River bridgehead, while in the centre the 324th Infantry held the line of the Blies and fought off three German attempts at crossing south-east of Habkirchen.

The mainspring of the German attack uncoiled furiously against the 71st Infantry Regiment, between Bliesbruck and Rimling. A five-company assault north of Rimling curled around the right flank of their 2nd Battalion, forcing a hurried 1,000-yard withdrawal. The 3rd Battalion moved up to the 2nd's assistance, but three companies of the enemy had already driven through the 1st Battalion on the left, penetrating the Bliesbrucken woods to a depth of 1 mile behind the American lines. The 3rd Battalion was diverted to meet the penetration and soon plunged into a savage battle in the forest. The thrust was stopped, but the Germans managed to hold on to the ground they had gained.

All day long the engagement swayed back and forth. Elements of the 2nd Battalion, supported by tanks, restored their original line by 0600 on January 1st only to be dislodged again at 0730. At nightfall the Battalion's right flank rested on a farm; the Germans attacked furiously during the night, setting the buildings on fire, and the Americans had to withdraw yet again. Finally, after mopping up isolated groups of the enemy in the woods, fresh American troops succeeded in establishing a new line and the battered 2nd Battalion went into reserve.

On January 3rd, the 71st Regiment's line was again attacked by a strong force of tanks and infantry. The situation was stabilised by the 3rd Battalion of the 253rd Infantry, assisted by the 2nd Battalion of the 114th, now attached to the 71st; but enemy groups continued to infiltrate around Aachen to attack the American flanks.. Units of the 255th Infantry and the 2nd French Armoured Division had to be hurriedly sent in to plug the gap.

Next day the last German remnants around Aachen were wiped out as the 2nd Battalion of the 255th cleared the town and units of the 71st Infantry attacked from the north. There was bitter fighting around Gross Rederching, where the Germans used captured Sherman tanks in a surprise attack which drove French armour from the town. An attempt to retake Gross Rederching by the 71st Infantry was also beaten off, but then the enemy disengaged abruptly. It was apparent that the Sarre pincer of Operation 'Nordwind' had failed.

Caught between the Sarre push of the German Attack Group I and Attack Group II's drive near Bitche was the 100th Infantry Division, holding the line from Rimling to Bitche. If this phase of the enemy offensive had gone according to plan, the division would almost certainly have been cut off; as it was, the German thrust south-east of Bitche exposed the division's right flank dangerously, forcing it to bend southward to meet the threat from the east and from what was, in effect, a second front, at right angles to the original one.

Meanwhile, on the left flank of VI Corps in the Low Vosges, Task Force

Hudelson was in desperate trouble. In the early hours of January 1st, its thinly stretched, 10-mile front was assailed by the 256th and 361st Volks Grenadier Divisions, launching a two-pronged assault south-eastwards from Bitche. There had been no artillery or mortar preparation, so the attack came without warning. The Americans fought off successive waves of enemy infantry until dawn, when they were finally overwhelmed. The haggard survivors, surrounded by the enemy, banded together in small groups in an attempt to break out of the trap.

To the east, the Allied lines were riddled by enemy penetration as the Americans fell back on Bannstein and maintained a perimeter defence there until 1130 on January 2nd. Over on the left flank of the task force, the 117th Cavalry Reconnaissance Squadron had been hit hard and virtually surrounded, but they managed to extricate themselves with heavy losses. On January 3rd, the Germans renewed their efforts to enlarge the Bitche Salient; infantry, tanks and artillery mingled in confused fighting all along the line. To the south-east, American forces detailed to clear Wingen had been forced to proceed more cautiously than usual; there were Allied prisoners-of-war in the town and the use of artillery was out of the question. But on January 6th, Wingen was finally cleared and the enemy's deepest penetration into the Vosges was eliminated.

The fact that the Allies had been aware of the impending German offensive had enabled them to regroup rapidly to contain the Bitche Salient. VI Corps held on grimly and traded blow for blow with the enemy, sapping its strength and taking the momentum out of its drive. According to the German Chief of Staff, who was with his troops on January 6th and 7th, the rugged terrain also imposed a severe strain on the men, who had few reserves or supplies and who had been fighting without respite since the offensive began. On both sides, troops had to sleep out in the open, snatching what fitful rest they could on wet ground in sodden, mud-caked uniforms.

As the German drive gradually lost its impetus, VI Corps stepped up its own offensive activity, slipping shock troops through breaks in the line to harass enemy communications. An intercepted enemy report revealed that the Germans were unable to exploit the Bitche Salient without substantial reinforcements. But they could hold it; the same terrain that had hampered the breakthrough attempt also hampered the Americans in their efforts to reduce the salient.

Some of the less favourable implications of the brilliant Allied drive on Strasbourg now became evident. On the northern front, the Low Vosges formed a 10-mile-wide barrier between the Allied forces to the east and west, making contact between the two sides difficult and penetration by a

Above: The 697th Field Artillery Battalion
unload powder charges for their 240mm
howitzers near Lorentzen, France, during the
German offensive Operation 'Nordwind'
designed to regain the Saverne Gap in
January, 1945.

Below: A huge convoy moves up to supply
the Seventh Army, which, at the end of
January, was winning the battle for Alsace.

strong enemy force relatively easy on the right flank. If the Germans were to strike here, it would be hard for the Americans to hold their ground on the swampy, wooded bank of the Rhine—and there was always the danger that the enemy might attempt to establish a bridgehead on the west bank, trapping a sizeable Allied force.

Adding to the problems was the big German bridgehead in the Colmar Pocket, which the First French Army had made little progress in eliminating by the end of December, 1944. The importance the Germans attached to maintaining a foothold here may be judged by the fact that during the first half of December they poured over 8,000 reinforcements into the Pocket—over 80 per cent of all the replacement troops flung against the Sixth Army Group during this period. Their ultimate aim was to deploy sufficient striking power in the Colmar Pocket to enable them to attack northwards, breaking through the French and creating yet another front for the already overstretched Seventh Army.

The Ardennes offensive in the north ruled out any possibility of the Seventh Army receiving powerful reserves to counter the menace. Nor was that all; on December 26th, Seventh Army itself had been ordered to earmark for SHAEF reserve one infantry division, an armoured division and a corps headquarters. Even on January 7th, when the German stabs at the Seventh Army's front were hurting a lot, reinforcements were allocated by SHAEF on a ratio of about eight for Twelfth Army Group to one for Sixth Army Group. All this meant that the Seventh Army lacked the strength to resist successfully throughout the line; all it could do was predict where the successive enemy thrusts would fall, try to blunt them with artillery fire and move its scant reserves hurriedly into positions where they would have the maximum effect in limiting enemy penetration.

The basic flaws in the Seventh Army's position led to the consideration of a planned withdrawal as a means of coping with a strong enemy offensive on more than one front. In fact, getting the Seventh out of the potential trap before the jaws were sprung seemed, at this stage, to be the only sensible course of action. Accordingly, on January 2nd, 1945, VI Corps was ordered to continue withdrawing to the main Vosges positions beyond the Maginot Line, a move to be completed by January 5th. These orders were amplified by General Jacob L. Devers, commanding Sixth Army Group, in a message to General Patch. He indicated that on the morning of January 2nd General Eisenhower had expressed concern that divisions in the Haguenau area might be badly mauled or cut off by a successful enemy drive south towards Sarrebourg or north from the Colmar Pocket. The Supreme Commander thought it advisable to maintain only minimum forces in this area, withdrawing the bulk of VI Corps behind the main

111

Vosges positions. Eisenhower went on to elaborate on the strategy that lay behind this decision:

"The Ardennes situation is not yet restored, thus making it imperative that a SHAEF reserve be available to move north at an early date. It is essential therefore that you form the local army and army group reserves with a minimum delay. Time is pressing and the necessity for these emergency measures must be realised by all concerned.'

The main defensive positions were therefore to be organised as quickly as possible, and in great depth. Covering forces in the Alsace Plain were to be provided with adequate motor transport to enable them to pull back rapidly in the face of strong German offensive action, destroying all crossing points in the process.

The Seventh Army's withdrawal was to be fully co-ordinated with that of the First French Army, with the main defensive hinge situated between the two armies at Obernai. The loss of Strasbourg and the territory east of the Vosges would be a bitter pill for the French to swallow, and they soon made their feelings known. On the morning of January 3rd, a French courier arrived at General Patch's HQ carrying a letter from General Schwartz, the French Military Governor of Strasbourg. Schwartz made an impassioned plea against the departure of Allied forces from Alsace, saying that it would probably lead to a wholesale massacre of the civilian population once the Germans returned.

General Devers also arrived at the Seventh Army's command post in Luneville that morning, and Patch informed him of Schwartz's objections. According to the Seventh Army diary, Devers "stated that Strasbourg would be evacuated in the course of the withdrawal and that the Commanding General, Seventh Army, would pay no attention to any pressure, political or otherwise, to continue to hold Strasbourg". Both the Commanding General and Chief of Staff of the Seventh Army once again stressed the concern of the French Government, expressed through General Schwartz. They also told Devers that Strasbourg could be included in a revised defensive line based on the Maginot Line and the area extending southwards from where the latter joined the Rhine. They pointed out that this line was already fortified, whereas the terrain to its rear was of indifferent defensive value. But Devers remained adamant; the orders were that Strasbourg would be abandoned.

Even as Devers and Patch were arguing, however, matters were taking a new turn. As a result of a personal plea from General de Gaulle, urging that Strasbourg should be defended and as much of Alsace as possible, General Eisenhower issued new instructions to Sixth Army Group at noon on the 3rd, giving it the responsibility for defending the city.

General Devers was still at the Seventh Army command post when the new SHAEF orders arrived, and immediately approved the earlier suggestion that VI Corps should hold the Maginot-Rhine line, with successive defensive lines to the rear in case a sudden withdrawal became necessary. Meanwhile, XV Corps would hang on to its present positions and stand ready to counter a possible enemy penetration.

VI Corps had begun the first of its major withdrawals twenty-four hours earlier, falling back on the Maginot Line positions between the Low Vosges and the Rhine. The move was scarcely completed when, on January 5th, an enemy battalion crossed the Rhine near Gambsheim, threatening the eastern flank of the Seventh Army salient in the Alsace Plain.

The German Nineteenth Army was using nine divisions against the French in a bid to develop the Colmar Pocket into a threat to Strasbourg from the south, and although the Seventh Army's stand at the turn of the year had frustrated enemy plans for a quick victory, the situation was still extremely dangerous. On January 8th, a Seventh Army directive called for the regrouping of VI, XV and XXI Corps, the latter newly released from SHAEF reserve. XXI Corps, under the command of Major-General Frank W. Milburn, became operational on January 13th, establishing liaison with the US Third Army on its left. The reshuffle assigned control of the 36th, 44th and 100th Infantry Divisions, Task Force Harris and the 2nd French Armoured Division to XV Corps, while VI Corps was assigned the 45th and 79th Infantry Divisions, the 12th and 14th Armoured Divisions and Task Forces Herren and Linden.

Later, captured German documents showed that as early as January 3rd the enemy had begun to plan for a second major offensive in the Sarre Valley, codenamed Operation 'Zahnarzt' (Dentist). However, the first Sarre offensive in the Bitche Salient had exhausted the German resources to such an extent that Generaloberst Blaskowitz, of Army Group G, admitted in a report dated January 8th that it would not be difficult for the Americans to regain the initiative. He recommended that High Command West should concentrate on the completion of Operation 'Nordwind', and postpone 'Zahnarzt' indefinitely. As a direct result of these recommendations, 'Zahnarzt' never went beyond the planning stage, and—except for one attack at Rimling—the Sarre sector stayed quiet for the rest of the month.

Meanwhile, the Low Vosges campaign developed into a battle for the control of roads and passes, with the Americans making little or no headway against the Bitche Salient. On the morning of January 14th, for example, the 157th Infantry relieved the 276th in the line and a few hours later launched an attack on strong enemy positions east of the road which the 276th had been holding. The American advance was immediately shrivelled up by intense artillery, Nebelwerfer and mortar fire; the 276th had apparently given away its positions and the fact that it was to be relieved by the 157th by sending radio messages in the clear, and when the 157th's attack eventually developed the Germans were ready and waiting. Only one battalion—the 3rd—could claim to have made any headway; this advanced 2,000 yards, halfway to its objectives, and captured two hills. However, both the 180th Infantry on the Battalion's left and the 1st Battalion of the 157th on its right were hopelessly pinned down, and with its flank unprotected the 3rd Battalion was soon in danger of encirclement by the 11th Regiment of the 6th SS Mountain Division.

The rest of the 157th Infantry fought desperately to reinforce the 3rd Battalion, and on January 15th the 2nd and 1st Battalions managed to gain some ground on the left and right—but only two companies, C and G, succeeded in making contact and in doing so they lost touch with their own Battalions, becoming part of the isolated force. The remaining units of the Regiment tried for five days to break through to the assistance of the isolated companies, which by then were completely encircled. Leaden, snow-filled skies frustrated plans to airdrop supplies, and well-camouflaged enemy strongpoints covered every trail.

On January 20th, after the failure of their fifth attempt to advance, the 157th was ordered to withdraw and word was sent to the five trapped companies to make a break for it. At 1530, the isolated men radioed: ''We're coming out. Give us everything you've got.'' The remainder of the 157th immediately opened up with a barrage of automatic fire which continued for three minutes, after which a smokescreen was laid to cover the breakout attempt. It was hopeless. An hour later, a desperate radio operator informed the 157th CP that the enemy cordon could not be broken. Two haggard, unshaven infantrymen managed to break through just before nightfall; they reported that all but 125 of the original force of 750 men had been killed or wounded.

Darkness came, and with it driving snow. Out of the murk, the tough SS troops launched their final assault, and the survivors of the five companies were overwhelmed. The next morning, the 157th Infantry was pulled out of the line.

Despite tragedies like this, the Americans resisted every German attempt to break out of the Bitche Salient, while in the Sarre Valley and the Low Vosges the enemy battered themselves into such a state of exhaustion that by January 20th the Allied communiques described the situation as 'stable'. Yet the Germans were still far from finished; on January 5th, the

Oberrhein Army Group had thrust their way across the Rhine at Gambsheim in conjunction with simultaneous attacks elsewhere, and counter-strokes in the Rhine Valley went on all through January as the enemy made their last desperate fling before being forced over to the defensive.

The Allied resistance on VI Corps Rhine flank had been complicated to no small extent by the rapid changes in policy over Strasbourg. Command of this area passed from the Seventh Army to the First French Army on January 5th. It was on that date that the Germans struck across the Rhine, with the result that the French were unable to assume any real control for two more days. When the enemy attacked between Kilstett and Drusenheim at 0745 that morning, the Seventh Army units in the vicinity of Strasbourg were in the throes of reorganisation, and the defence was essentially a makeshift one. Two task forces countered the assault as best they could. At 1545 Task Force A attacked astride the road from Weyersheim to Gambsheim; the Americans were held up by accurate automatic fire at a canal, but troops on the right flank forced a crossing and reached a creek between the canal and Gambsheim. However, with the onset of darkness, they lost contact and were compelled to withdraw west of the canal for regrouping. Task Force B was also held up by heavy artillery fire north of Kilstett.

As soon as he learned of the German attack, the VI Corps Commander, General Brooks, put through an urgent telephone call to General Wyche, commanding the 79th Division: "Get in there and get it cleaned up—it's got to be cleaned up pronto . . . we can't let it get built up there."

It was, however, easier said than done. The Germans quickly established a bridgehead 5 miles long and 2 miles deep and their build-up was continuing; snuffing out their assault was going to be a lengthy business. On the morning of January 6th, Task Force A battered its way into Gambsheim and cleared the main part of the town after some vicious house-to-house fighting, but General Wyche nevertheless had to inform Brooks that things were not going too well. "The real trouble is this mushroom organisation plus the greenness of the troops and lack of communications . . . I'm very sorry to have to present this situation, but that's the way it is."

On January 7th, according to captured documents, the Oberrhein High Command received direct orders from Hitler to lighten the task of Army Group G—which was conducting the general offensive in Alsace—by exerting steady pressure from the Gambsheim bridgehead and exploiting the gains already made south of Strasbourg. The latter push, however, was contained by the French armour, and by January 16th there was no longer strong pressure in this sector.

Above: M-10 tank destroyers, serving as artillery, fire on the Germans in the Colmar Pocket, which, by the end of January the Seventh Army was beginning to liquidate.

Below: A convoy of Seventh Army ambulances winds through the Vosges mountains near Ribeauville on its way to the front line in Alsace.

The American armour suffered heavily in the fighting around the Gambsheim bridgehead. At Herlisheim, American units became encircled and armour was dispatched to break through to them early on January 10th. Soon afterwards, the tank battalion commander radioed that "things were pretty hot". It was the last message he ever sent; thirty minutes later fourteen of the twenty-nine Shermans engaged were smouldering on the edge of the town, and his was one of them. The troops in Herlisheim managed to break out that afternoon.

The next German push in the Herlisheim area came on January 19th, when the 10th SS Panzer Division came into conflict with the 12th Armoured Division. At 1630, enemy infantry supported by ten tanks secured the bridge over the canal and began to cross, but eight of them were quickly knocked out by American artillery and the attack shrivelled up. Fifteen minutes later, an estimated 200 German infantry and 17 tanks crossed the Zorn River at Herlisheim and raced north-westwards, while at 1715 400 men and 17 tanks crossed the bridge over the canal, this time successfully. Fierce fighting raged all night, and the tide began to turn in the Americans's favour only at dawn, when rocket-firing Thunderbolts of the XII TAF appeared overhead. In all the American pilots flew 16 missions totalling 190 sorties, destroying 27 enemy tanks. Despite the hammering it had received, the 10th Panzer Division's punch had carried enough weight to force the 12th Armoured back to a defensive line between Weyersheim and Rohrwiller; by this time the Division was 1,200 men under strength and had lost 70 vehicles, and the 36th Division was rushed into the line to lift the pressure.

In fact, combat efficiency reports for the six regular divisions in VI Corps on January 19th showed that only two, the 36th and 163rd, merited a 'very satisfactory' rating. Three were described as 'satisfactory' and one, the 12th Armoured, 'unsatisfactory'. Every division was suffering badly from combat fatigue; and, when it became obvious that the enemy was gathering his forces for a fresh onslaught, General Patch informed General Devers that VI Corps could not hold the front as it existed. Devers at once ordered a further withdrawal, and this immediately placed the Germans at a tactical disadvantage. Apart from having to waste ammunition against diminishing Allied troop concentrations, they also had to follow up the withdrawal—hampered all the way by obstacles and small-scale delaying actions. Then they had to locate the new Allied line and move up supplies, a laborious process because of the poor road network and severe icing. The weather conditions troubled the Americans too, but they managed to establish their new line at the Moder River on the night of January 20th/21st. As VI Corps enjoyed its first breathing space for some time,

Patch observed to Brooks: "I think the enemy is getting a little tired. I think we will be able to hang on all right."

On January 21st, while the other VI Corps units were settling into the Moder Line, the 36th Division had a head-on clash with the Germans as the latter probed for a weak spot through which to inject tanks and infantry. Fifteen enemy tanks launched a powerful thrust at noon, but American tank destroyers and artillery knocked several out and the remainder retreated. A second attack by a dozen tanks was also beaten off in the afternoon, and 100 German troops who worked their way into the American positions near Kurzenhausen were quickly surrounded and mopped up.

The following day, the German Army Group G received orders to attack Lower Alsace, and if possible push on towards Saverne. The attack was to be continued as long as there was any hope of destroying the Americans north of the Haguenau-Saverne line or forcing them to retreat beyond the Saverne Gap, permitting a link-up with the German Nineteenth Army in the Colmar Pocket.

The plans looked clear-cut enough on paper, but they had taken little account of the weather. On the morning of the 23rd, heavy snow began to fall; by the end of the week it was over 1ft deep, with temperatures falling to 15° below zero. The following afternoon the snow lifted a little, and the Luftwaffe took advantage of the break in the weather by sending twenty-plus Focke-Wulf 190s and Junkers 88s to strafe the 36th Division's area. The air attack in fact heralded the ground offensive, which unrolled on the night of January 24th/25th in bitter cold and driving snow, with six German divisions thrusting towards the Moder in a three-pronged assault. The enemy planned to capture Strasbourg by January 30th—the twelfth anniversary of Hitler's rise to power—and they threw everything they had into the attack. The 6th SS Mountain Division enjoyed some initial success, driving through thin resistance by the 103rd Division to take Schillersdorf while the 36th Volks Grenadiers maintained pressure on the 103rd elsewhere. The third prong of the offensive stabbed into the eastern foothills of the Low Vosges at Kaltenhause—but the Germans never really gained the initiative. Although sizeable forces got across the Moder in assault craft, an attempt to isolate Haguenau with a pincer movement was smashed after some fierce fighting in the snow.

By nightfall on the 25th, it was already obvious that the Allied line was not going to break. Moreover, the day's fighting had cost the Germans heavy losses, and to sustain their push they had been compelled to inject substantial reinforcements—men who could ill be spared from the West Wall defences.

118

The price was too high. A few hours later, on the orders of Hitler himself, Army Group G suspended its offensive operations in the Lower Vosges and Alsace.

Meanwhile, the Colmar Pocket—where a sizeable enemy force still held on with its back to the Rhine between Strasbourg and Mulhouse—had become quite an embarrassment to the Allies and in particular to the First French Army, which had proved incapable of making inroads into this, the Germans's last foothold on French soil. On January 15th, the French had been ordered to: "Launch without delay and by surprise, with all the means now at your disposal, powerful offensive operations converging in the direction of Brisach and aimed at total reduction of the Alsace Bridgehead." However, it was to be another week before the French were in anything like a fit state to undertake such a task.

The assault was to be spearheaded by the French I Corps, which was to strike on a narrow front with everything it had and so, it was hoped, achieve a decisive breakthrough. The thrust got under way at 0800 on January 20th, right on schedule—but the jump-off was just about the only thing destined to go as planned during the following two weeks. After eleven days of fighting in the worst weather imaginable, the Corps had failed to reach a single one of its objectives. The infantry had reached the limit of their endurance, the armour was cut to half its original strength by enemy action and mechanical troubles, and repair and recovery crews were dropping like flies from exhaustion. On January 31st, at the end of its tether, the entire Corps undertook no offensive action of any kind and the men snatched whatever rest they could.

The next day, somewhat refreshed, I Corps managed to make a little headway against stiff enemy opposition, which included heavy artillery and minefields. The advance continued slowly on February 2nd, and that afternoon the American XXI Corps—attacking from the north-west—entered Colmar. On the 3rd, I Corps reached Ensisheim, its initial objective; the 2nd Moroccan Division encountered a strong enemy force in the Nonnebruch Woods and shattered it, providing I Corps with a firm base for a drive north to join up with XXI Corps at Rouffach.

The attack on the northern flank of the Colmar Pocket by the US XXI Corps, in conjunction with units of the French II Corps, began on the night of January 22nd/23rd with the US 3rd Infantry Division, the 5th French Armoured and the 1st Moroccan Infantry in the vanguard. Opposing this force were some 25 enemy battalions, each with about 500 men. The 7th and 30th Infantry Regiments began the assault, crossing the Fecht River on a footbridge and fanning out across the Colmar Forest towards the Ill River crossings. Both regiments met scattered strongpoints, mines, wire entanglements and heavy small-arms fire, and the men had to struggle through deep snow. Casualties suffered horribly; in those freezing conditions, even a flesh wound was agonising.

The Moroccans reached the Ill at dawn and crossed it, although not without losing many men from the hundreds of plastic mines scattered over the snow-covered ground. While the French were fighting their way across the Ill, the 1st Battalion of the 7th Infantry battled its way into Ostheim. The attack was opposed by enemy armour, but, after several tanks had been knocked out with bazookas, the town was finally secured at noon.

Meanwhile, the 30th Infantry had also crossed the Ill and were preparing to push on towards the Colmar Canal. Here the Germans launched a strong counter-attack, supported by tanks. The US troops called for armour and a force of Shermans quickly appeared on the scene. Then came disaster: as the leading tank rumbled on to the bridge across the Ill, the structure collapsed, cutting off further support from the infantry on the other side. All the GIs could do was hold on, beat off successive German attacks as best they could, and pray that the bridging engineers could work a miracle.

At 2030 that same day—January 23rd—the 3rd Division's commander, General O'Daniel, ordered the commander of the 30th Infantry to "take over the attack with the same objectives . . . plan is now to hold bridgehead and line along the Ill River. We will get bridge that tank fell thru back in, send armour across and attack again."

A Bailey Bridge was completed by 0730 the next morning. A force of American tanks at once moved across, only to be met by a withering 88mm fire which knocked out several of them. A few minutes later, German tanks emerged from Riedwihr Forest and engaged the survivors. A furious tank and artillery duel raged across the Colmar Plain throughout the whole of that day, with smoke staining the sky from the burnt-out carcases of Shermans and Mk IVs.

It was during the battles of the 23rd that the French First Army suffered some of its heaviest casualties. Its infantry strength was so depleted at the end of the day's fighting that General de Lattre addressed a plea to Eisenhower, through General Devers, for an American division to bolster the flagging French infantry. On the 27th, XXI corps was ordered to take over part of the French sector, and twenty-four hours later it launched an attack towards Neuf-Brisach in a bid to cut off the German escape route from Colmar. From the north, the remainder of XXI Corps battered its way towards Colmar through bitter rearguard opposition, and on February 2nd Shermans of the 5th French Armoured Division rumbled into the town to a tumultuous reception.

Driving on southwards, the Allied forces occupied Hat-statt and at 0200 on February 5th moved on towards Rouffach. Several enemy units were by-passed and trapped on the Rouffach road to be mopped up later. The Allied infantry made short work of enemy road-blocks and entered Rouffach at 0512 that same morning. Meanwhile other troops circled the town to seal off the exits and make contact with units of the French I Corps, which had reached the southern outskirts during the night.

The junction of XXI Corps and I Corps meant that the Colmar Pocket was effectively split in two. Enemy resistance began to crumble rapidly now; in the north the 3rd, 28th and 75th Divisions advanced on the Rhine, overcoming isolated groups of battle-weary Germans en route, and later the 3rd Division drove southwards between the Rhône-Rhine Canal and the Rhine itself.

Patrols from the 1st Battalion of the 30th Infantry reconnoitred the walled town of Neuf-Brisach during the night of February 5th/6th, and at first light struck southward towards it. A short time later, the Americans had a real windfall when they captured a civilian who claimed to know of a secret way into the fortress. It turned out to be a low-ceilinged, 60ft tunnel leading under the walls from the dry moat outside. A platoon of infantry went cautiously through, led by the civilian; they found only seventy-six German soldiers still within and these were cleared by mid-morning. Prisoners told the Americans that their officers had exhorted them to resist to the last man—but the officers themselves were significantly absent when Neuf-Brisach fell.

After scattered mopping-up operations on February 8th, XXI Corps was in control of all the territory assigned to it. By that time, too, the French I Corps to the south had practically completed its annihilation of the German forces still remaining in the pocket. Units of the Corps, supported by armour, herded the last few Germans in Alsace into a very small bridgehead at Chalampe, away to the south-east. On February 9th the enemy abandoned this last foothold west of the Rhine and crossed the river, blowing the bridge behind them. The Wehrmacht's last gamble was at an end.

X

The entire German withdrawal from the Colmar Pocket had been influenced by two major factors; high-level indecision in the early stages and the continuing importance of tying down the largest number of Allied troops for as long as possible. On January 27th, the German Commander-in-Chief West had been empowered "to withdraw the weakly-held Ill front to a straight line between the Ill and the Rhine, and beyond the Rhine as soon as defences had been erected". A ferry service had been planned to augment the flow of traffic across the bridge at Brisach, and work was also going ahead on three heavy and two light cable tracks over the river. But while the Führer approved the withdrawal of the Nineteenth Army's right wing, he instructed the Commander-in-Chief West to examine "to what extent the front of the Nineteenth Army could be improved by pressing forward the main line of resistance along the axis Selestat-Col du Bonhomme-Le Valtin, using the 6th SS Mountain Division for this purpose".

On January 29th, C-in-C West indicated that such an attack would be impracticable; the 6th SS Mountain Division could not be released from the First Army "in view of the large-scale attack expected against the Moselle Gap". It was, in fact, doubtful if the SS Division was still capable of carrying out a major assault. C-in-C West felt it more important to strengthen the army bridgehead on its present front, and the next day he issued orders stressing that it was essential to keep the bridgehead active and to pin down the enemy forces.

Late on January 31st, the German commander described the situation in the bridgehead as tense. By this time the maximum width of the bridgehead had been reduced to 25 miles and the Allies were only 5 miles from the bridge at Brisach. The dilemma facing the Germans was that both the First and Nineteenth Armies were badly under strength for the tasks confronting them; the First was momentarily expecting a large-scale

American assault on the Moselle front; and, since the Nineteenth's bridgehead had been all but wiped out, C-in-C West suggested that all German forces be withdrawn immediately from Alsace and sent to reinforce the First Army.

Within twenty-four hours, however, C-in-C West received orders in which Hitler refused to sanction the evacuation of the bridgehead. Units still in the pocket were to be deployed to meet attacks in the Colmar and Cernay-Mulhouse sectors; the Vosges sector was to be only lightly held. On the next day—February 2nd—while the Germans were discussing these top-level orders, news came through that Allied forces had entered Colmar. High Command West reported that the destruction of the Nineteenth Army would be inevitable if it were left west of the Rhine, and this would have disastrous consequences for the plans for building strong defences on the east bank. The Vosges bulge, weakened as it was by constant troop reshuffles in favour of the Colmar front, would easily be crushed by the Allied steamroller; a breakthrough at Colmar therefore seemed highly probable, and the Germans had no reinforcements available to stem the flood.

Finally, on February 3rd, High Command West received belated permission to evacuate the bridgehead. By the time this approval was granted, the 708th Infantry Division had already begun its withdrawal across the Rhine, while the 16th and 189th Volks Grenadier Divisions were both in the process of breaking off contact with the Allies. Five days later, High Command West reported that there were no longer "sufficient German forces in the bridgehead to hinder enemy operations".

By February 10th, 1945, the German Nineteenth Army—consisting of LXIV and LXIII Corps—had suffered over 22,000 casualties, as well as the loss of 55 armoured vehicles and 66 artillery pieces. LXIV Corps, comprising the 2nd Mountain Division, the 198th Infantry Division and the 189th, 708th and 16th Volks Grenadier Divisions, had taken a heavy beating; the 2nd Division alone suffered 1,000 combat casualties and lost 4,700 men taken prisoner. Of the three Volks Grenadier Divisions, the 189th came off worst, having been badly mauled in the defence of Colmar, and only the 708th managed to cross the Rhine more or less intact, having started its withdrawal on February 3rd. The 198th Infantry managed to extricate about 500 fighting troops; more than 1,000 more were taken prisoner.

In the southern sector, LXIII Corps had also been severely handled. Not more than 400 combat troops of the 338th Infantry Division succeeded in getting away from the Vosges area; 1,750 were made prisoner. The 159th Volks Grenadier Division abandoned Cernay after a fight that cost it 800 men killed or wounded and 1,200 prisoners, while the 716th Division lost at least 426 dead and 800 captured in its determined defensive action north of Mulhouse.

The forces which did struggle clear across the Rhine were mostly deployed along the east bank opposite the former pocket. Some units were absorbed into First Army divisions which were desperately short of replacements. Both the 2nd Mountain Division and the 338th Division were transferred to the northern front in support of the First Army, now marshalling its strength to take the shock of yet another impending offensive by the US Seventh Army. For the Allies, the last lap was about to begin.

After the failure of the enemy attack across the Moder River on January 25th, the Seventh Army began to regain the initiative which was to carry it through to the end of the war. Having secured the Sixth Army Group's northern flank during the reduction of the Colmar Pocket, it now remained for the Seventh to straighten its front and ensure a clean line of departure for the coming Allied offensive.

The 36th Division had been scheduled to clear an area on the Moder line on January 30th, but a sudden thaw made the ground too soft for heavy vehicles and the attack was postponed for twenty-four hours. Soon after 2100 on the 31st, the 2nd Battalion of the 142nd Infantry crossed the river and moved into Oberhoffen; the only enemy opposition was an isolated machine-gun post, which was successfully dealt with at 0330. Meanwhile, the 141st Infantry had established a twenty-eight-man strongpoint on the Zorn River west of Herlisheim, while the 117th Reconnaissance Squadron probed for a bridgehead on the south-east side. The following morning, the 1st Battalion of the 142nd Infantry also crossed the Moder to join the 2nd in Oberhoffen. During the two days of operations, artillery fire on both sides had been severely limited by a critical ammunition shortage; the 36th Division's artillery, for example, was rationed to a mere eleven rounds a day!

Four days of exceptionally mild weather had melted 1ft of snow, flooding the lowlands laying across the Seventh Army's attack route and generally softening up all the ground. Footbridges across the Moder were washed out completely. During the night of February 1st/2nd, American troops pushed deep into the Drusenheim woods, but they were unable to dislodge a force of Germans occupying a wooded section of the Rohrwiller-Drusenheim road. Two battalions of the 143rd Regiment sloshed through 3ft of water to attack Rohrwiller; they had a sharp fight with units of the 10th SS Panzer Division and took 210 prisoners, but their own casualties were considerably higher. The trouble was that the US infantry lacked

Above: Units of the 63rd Infantry Division arrive at Sarrebourg in France after a long trip from the USA via Marseilles. Later they moved up to join other Seventh Army troops massing for the drive into Germany in February, 1945.

Below: A machine-gun crew advances under covering fire on the 63rd Division's front at Sarreguemines during the Seventh Army's drive across the German border in February, 1945.

armoured support; the few tanks that tried to cross the waterlogged fields were bogged down in a matter of yards.

The approach march on Herlisheim by two companies of the 3rd Battalion, 141st Infantry, began at 0300 on February 3rd in torrential rain, the troops wading through waist-deep water. In the darkness and the blinding rain, the Americans stumbled into the outskirts of Herlisheim without realising it, but the Germans were on the alert and the leading GIs were immediately mown down by machine-gun fire. Shots were exchanged throughout the rest of the night, but as neither side could see the other the shooting was haphazard. As soon as they could see the outlines of the houses in the greyness of dawn, the Americans got under cover and waited for armoured support for an attack on the town, but the Shermans never came. When tanks did appear, they were German—and the Americans were forced to fall back towards Weyersheim.

The 36th Division's 'limited objective' attack during the early part of February, 1945 was the only offensive operation of any importance attempted on the Moder River front before the beginning of the big stab at the Siegfried Line and the Saar-Palatinate in the middle of March. VI Corps settled down to a period of relative quiet. Further west, however, from the Low Vosges to St Avold, XV and later XXI Corps continued to engage the enemy in a series of actions designed to prepare the ground for the March assault.

By the end of January, the Germans had begun to transfer some of their more experienced units to Russia and the principal Western Front further north, and the western flank of the Seventh Army—west of the Low Vosges and in the Sarre Valley—lapsed into a state of static defence. By February 10th, all identified German reserves in the Saar-Palatinate had departed. During the fighting in the Colmar Pocket, units of XV Corps had maintained their positions and carried out a programme of aggressive patrolling in order to keep a firm hold of the initiative—not an easy task in weather conditions varying from the bitter cold and heavy snow of January to February's unexpected deluge.

The Corps's offensive operations in mid-February were designed to straighten out 'sags' in the line at Gross Rederching and Welferding. The divisions involved were the 44th, 63rd and 100th. While the 44th was assigned a line between Rimling and Epping-Urbach to the northern fringes of the eastern part of the Bliesbrucken woods, the 63rd Division's 255th Infantry was to launch a simultaneous attack on the central sector of the woods. The 100th Division was to push its left flank forward on the 44th's right.

Patrols during the preceding weeks had revealed that although the southern edge of the area was heavily mined and wired and had many strongpoints, the eastern and western fringes were either unguarded at night or were weakly held. The 44th Division jumped-off an hour before dawn on February 15th. The 324th Infantry quickly outflanked the Buchenbusch woods on both sides, moving stealthily through the pre-dawn shadows. As dawn broke, the Americans opened up a withering fire from the Germans's flanks and rear, taking them completely by surprise and forcing them back towards their own mines and wire. By mid-morning, 161 prisoners had been taken and the 324th's objective was secure.About the same time the 71st Infantry and the 749th Tank Battalion—attacking in the centre—occupied Rimling after overcoming only moderate resistance.

On the 44th Division's left, it was a different story; in this sector the enemy fought with tigerish ferocity, and the 114th Infantry—which reached the northern edge of the woods by noon—was soon in trouble. The Germans had turned two farms into heavily-defended strongpoints, and although many of the buildings had been destroyed by US artillery fire they still provided plenty of cover for riflemen and machine-gunners. Companies of the 38th Panzer Grenadier Regiment were well dug in around the farms, protected by rings of anti-personnel mines.

The American plan was to by-pass the farms and then assault them from the rear. Only a small combat patrol was to advance directly against the first farm, Bellevue, to divert the enemy's attention. The point patrol, however, was quickly pinned down by highly accurate machine-gun fire from the ruins, and Company G, attempting to slip past to the west, was also stopped dead in its tracks at the expense of several men killed and wounded. Company E came up in support, but despite repeated attempts both companies could get no closer to the farm than the edge of Bliesbrucken woods. Company E's effort was then switched towards the other farm, Brandelfingerhoff, the buildings of which sprawled over a wider area and were therefore less readily defensible. This farm was taken after a stiff fight at 1300, but it was another hour before Bellevue fell. Rocket-firing Thunderbolts of XII TAF flew two strikes against the farm, which was eventually captured by Company F while Company G provided covering fire. The battle for the two farms had cost the Americans 145 men killed and wounded; the Germans suffered 100 casualties, with 129 men taken prisoner.

By 1500, the 44th Division had secured all its objectives and the surviving Germans withdrew to the north. The enemy, however, was not yet completely beaten; early the next morning they launched two counter-attacks. The first, which came at 0320—just as the exhausted GIs were trying to snatch a few hours' sleep—was broken up by artillery fire

Above: After eliminating a German pillbox with white phosphorous and smoke grenades, a squad leaves cover to clear another strongpoint. The 63rd Division troops of the Seventh Army were straightening out sags in the line at Gross Rederching and Welferding preparatory to advancing into Germany.

Below: Just after the battle had passed on and the Seventh Army had entered Germany, troops of the 71st Infantry Regiment march through the ruins of the French border town of Rimling.

before it had time to develop fully, but at 0530 200 enemy troops supported by 10 armoured vehicles smashed into the 71st Regiment's lines and were only beaten off after a heavy fight.

To the west of the 44th, the 255th Infantry of the 63rd Division had had a difficult time tackling the centre of the Bliesbruchen woods. The main effort here was made by the 3rd Battalion, which had been assigned the task of seizing and consolidating high ground in the woods north of the railroad track under cover of supporting fire from the 1st Battalion. At 0615 on the 15th, Companies I and K groped their way towards the objective through mist and darkness, guided by the flashes of the enemy guns. It was a nightmare journey; as the men clawed a path through thick, tangled undergrowth, the hail of small-arms fire detonated anti-personnel mines scattered among the trees, causing many casualties.

The German bunkers were sturdily constructed affairs of earth and logs against which small-arms fire and hand grenades were ineffective. Even bazooka rockets made little impression. Once again, it was up to the infantry; worming their way forward in small groups, they pushed right through the enemy field of fire, encircling each bunker in turn and throwing grenades into the tunnel-like entrances at the rear. As well as having to contend with fire from the bunkers, the GIs also had to beat off constant attacks by enemy infantry, some of whom wore American uniforms. By noon, Company I had managed to advance only 300 yards beyond its jump-off point before being pinned down again; Company K was more fortunate, advancing methodically in short rushes through intense rifle fire until a final effort secured the objective at 1130. A flanking assault on the remaining enemy positions by Company B at 1925 was brought to an abrupt halt by a barrage of rockets and murderous machine-gun fire, but at first light the following morning a combined assault by Companies B, I and L took the high ground and held it.

The next phase of the limited Allied offensive—a strong push by the 63rd Division's 253rd Infantry and the 70th Division against the Welferding salient on the western part of XV Corps's front—got under way two days after the 44th Division's successful drive in the Gross Rederching sector. As a diversionary measure, two small-scale attacks—codenamed 'Portland' and 'Seattle'—were carried out in the early hours of February 17th. At 0200, a patrol from Company E of the 253rd Infantry slipped across the Blies River in rubber assault craft and at 0600 made a surprise attack on the village of Babkirchen. The patrol returned to base an hour later with eleven prisoners. Meanwhile, a lieutenant and seventeen men of Company B had also crossed the river and were moving on Bliesbruck. In the wake of a 120-second artillery barrage, they rushed into the town,

129

hurling phosphorous and fragmentation grenades in all directions and spraying anything that moved with sub-machine-gun fire. They killed over a score of the enemy before withdrawing, bringing one prisoner out with them; their own casualties were three men wounded.

The main push was started at 0200 that same morning by the 2nd Battalion of the 253rd Infantry, moving out towards enemy positions brilliantly lit by the 353rd Searchlight Battalion. The 2nd fought its way through moderate resistance to Auersmacher, which was captured during the morning after four hours of house-to-house combat. Meanwhile, a fifteen-minute artillery barrage had paved the way for a thrust across the Blies by the 3rd Battalion. The heavy shelling exploded hundreds of anti-personnel mines on the opposite bank and blasted a path through the enemy's barbed-wire. As it lifted, the 3rd Battalion stormed across the river in assault craft and over a wooden assault bridge erected in just forty-five minutes by the 263rd Engineer Battalion. The Battalion reached its initial objectives and dug in, fighting off a German counter-attack during the afternoon.

The last action of this phase came after a five-day lapse, during which the Americans consolidated their newly-won positions. The objectives were the towns of Bubingen and Bliesransbach, including the high ground between them. On February 24th, the 253rd Infantry, supported by the 254th, stormed the towns and uplands and took them against only slight opposition. This finally eliminated the Welferding salient.

The Seventh Army's push had once again taken it across the German frontier. Settled astride the ridges and hills of northern Lorraine, the 70th Division faced the outer defences of the Siegfried Line. Before them spread a range of unevenly wooded hills, sown with 'dragon's teeth' and other fortifications guarding the approaches to Germany. The Division was now faced with the formidable task of battering its way through multiple belts of entrenchments and bunkers and across antitank ditches to seize the heights along the Sarre River south and south-west of Saarbrücken. Possession of the heights, and of the town itself, were both vital to the projected Seventh Army offensive against the main Seigfried Line defences.

One minute after midnight on February 17th, the 276th Infantry of 70th Division moved out in dense fog towards the first group of hills. After a few hundred yards, they were pinned down by heavy fire from self-propelled guns; they immediately dug in and waited for armoured support, but because of heavily mined roads it was several hours before the tanks were able to get through. By the end of the day, the entire divisional front had moved forward about 1 mile, the Americans taking 198 prisoners. The whole operation was hampered by fog, rain and clinging mud. Armoured vehicles became hopelessly trapped in the mire and had to be temporarily abandoned, their crews fighting on foot alongside the infantry.

The American advance ground on laboriously. On the 18th, the 276th Infantry came up against what appeared to be a formidable obstacle: the Schlossberg, an ancient castle of red stone perched on the rocky summit of a hill and framed by dark pine woods. The Americans had no idea how well the castle was defended; all they knew was that behind its 10ft thick walls the enemy had located an observation post for mortars and artillery. The position was well chosen, for it commanded an excellent view of the next Allied objective—the town of Forbach.

On the morning of February 19th, with two hills in the area already taken, Company I of the 276th moved up towards the Schlossberg. The troops approached the massive castle stealthily, through the surrounding trees, eyeing the great walls with something akin to awe and expecting all hell to break loose at any moment. But nothing happened; not a shot was fired. When the Americans scaled the walls they found the castle deserted, yet for some reason every man felt strangely uneasy.

It was not long before they found a reason for their doubts. Shortly after dark, without warning, German 88mm guns and mortars opened up an accurate and intense fire on the castle. Under cover of this barrage, enemy troops appeared from nowhere and stormed the outer perimeter of the Company's hastily erected defences. It was clear that Company I had fallen into a well-prepared trap. As the furious barrage lifted, the Germans rushed the castle from all sides. Accurate small-arms fire bowled many over like rabbits but the rest came on, tearing their way through gaps in the American wire. As the Germans raced towards the castle walls, the Americans played their only trump card, calling down friendly mortar and artillery fire on their own defensive area. 81mm mortar bombs and shells from the 884th Field Artillery Battalion erupted among the attackers, just a few yards short of Company I's positions. The counter-barrage came as a shock to the Germans, who had not expected having to attack through external artillery fire. They broke and ran, leaving many dead and wounded on the slopes behind them.

With the Schlossberg firmly secured, the Americans were free to turn their attention to Forbach. The town was bombed and shelled for ninety minutes, then units of the 274th and 276th Infantry probed into the outskirts shortly before midnight. Stiff resistance brought the American drive to a halt, and tanks were unable to manoeuvre effectively in the darkness and narrow streets; there was no alternative but to dig in and wait

Infantrymen of the XV Corps cross the river
Blies on footbridges while engineers construct
a Bailey bridge to carry armour. They were
taking part in Operation 'Undertone', the
Seventh Army's offensive against the Saar-
Palatinate in March, 1945.

for the dawn. The waiting was grim; the rattle of Spandaus split the darkness and the American positions came under continual fire from 88mm and 105mm guns sited east of the town. Dawn, when it came, was grey and miserable, with drizzle falling through a blanket of thick fog. In the murk the battle for Forbach went on, house by house, street by street, throughout the day. Fighter-bombers of XII TAF swooped low over the ruined streets whenever the fog lifted enough to permit an air strike, pounding enemy strongpoints with rockets. The enemy retreated to the basements of the ruined buildings and carried on the fight from there, and it was not until after nightfall on the 20th that the last pocket of resistance was mopped up.

By the end of February, the 70th Division had successfully completed the first phase of its attack in the Sarre Basin, having penetrated the primary German defences in front of the Siegfried Line and gained a foothold on German soil just south of Saarbrücken. In eleven days of offensive operations, the Division had taken more than 1,800 prisoners; its own casualties totalled 1,662, including 207 killed and 231 missing. After Forbach, the 274th Infantry pushed rapidly on to Stiring-Wendel, occupying the town on March 5th and liberating nearly a thousand Russians, Poles, French, Czechs and Yugoslavs from a German POW hospital. Some of the inmates had been captives for five years and were in pitiful shape.

Meanwhile, to the north-west, the Third Army had begun its penetration of the Palatinate, stepping up the threat to the enemy forces holding the Siegfried Line in front of XXI Corps. On March 13th, patrols reported a marked decrease in enemy activity in this sector, and orders were issued to pursue the Germans to the line of the Sarre River between Saarbrücken and Völklingen; this would bring XXI, XV and VI Corps to a line running from Schaffhausen and Hostenbach on the Sarre south-eastwards through Haguenau to Oberhoffen, where the Americans joined forces with the First French Army on the Rhine.

The Third and Seventh Armies now faced a triangular 'island', the Saar-Palatinate, defined by the Rhine to the east, the Moselle to the north-west and the Lauter-Sarre river line to the south-west. This area—the second richest industrial region on the western front—had four main terrain features: the Rhine Valley, the Hardt Mountains, the Saarbrücken-Kaiserslautern-Worms Corridor and the Hunsrück Mountains.

The Allied offensive against the Saar-Palatinate—codenamed Operation 'Undertone'—was launched on schedule on March 15th at 1945. XXI Corps and the 3rd and 45th Divisions of XV Corps jumped-off at 0100 hours; the main body of VI Corps attacked at 0645 and the 3rd Algerian

Above: Sherman tanks of the 100th Infantry
Division enter the Maginot fortress town of
Bitche after many months of siege during
final operations to clear the Saar-Palatinate by
the Seventh Army in March, 1945.

Below: A Seventh Army tank destroyer,
awaiting action, lies concealed in the ruined
outskirts of Rimling.

Infantry Division, under the operational command of VI Corps, moved out along the Rhine at 0715.

XV Corps was scheduled to play a central part in the Seventh Army's offensive, and was to make its main effort along the axis Rimling-Zweibrücken-Homberg-Kaiserslautern. It was also assigned the task of reducing the Maginot fortress town of Bitche. The bulk of the Seventh Army's divisions had been assigned to XV Corps for the offensive; two recent arrivals were the advance detachment of the 71st Infantry Division, under Major-General Willard G. Wyman, and the 6th Armoured Division commanded by Major-General Robert W. Grow.

The assault at 0100 was preceded by an intense bombardment by aircraft of RAF Bomber Command and American artillery, aimed principally at enemy communications on the east bank of the Blies River, XV Corps's initial objective. The Blies varied in width from 75-144ft, with a depth of up to 15ft; American reconnaissance patrols had already selected suitable footbridge and ferry sites, while assault craft had been brought up and the banks cleared of mines. The 45th Division went in first. By 0235, four companies of the 180th Infantry were safely across; the bulk of the Regiment began to cross fifteen minutes later over two footbridges erected by the 120th Engineer Battalion. At dawn the leading units of the 45th were penetrating the forward enemy positions; the 180th Infantry subsequently drove northwards along the west bank of the Blies and the 157th pushed ahead on the right, while the task of mopping-up fell to the 179th Regiment. The first day of the offensive went exactly according to plan; the Germans seemed unable to recover from the initial surprise, falling back steadily on the main concrete and steel fortifications of the Siegfried Line, and the Americans took 628 prisoners.

Meanwhile, in a parallel assault codenamed Operation 'Earthquake', the 3rd Division had also launched an attack at 0100 on the 15th near Rimling. Within half an hour, the Americans had crossed into German territory and overrun the forward enemy defences. They had to negotiate minefields, which, though dense, did not extend for more than a mile in depth. Only at Ottweiler was there any serious German resistance—and in fact the 2nd Battalion of the 7th Infantry was encircled here for a while—but armoured support arrived quickly, knocking out four enemy Flakwagons and seven tank destroyers.

On the right flank of XV Corps, the 100th Division had begun its assault on Bitche at 0500 on the 15th. The 100th had fought over this same ground in December, and GIs who had experienced the vicious battle for the Maginot Line forts were apprehensive. Three infantry regiments were involved. The 397th Infantry poured out to take the high ground north of the fortress and captured Schorbach by noon, the 399th attacked Reyersviller Ridge and the 398th seized Forts Freudenberg and Schiesseck by frontal assault. The troops were relieved to meet only moderate resistance; the division's engineers had done their work well in December and the sector's main defences were still out of action. The greatest danger, in fact, came from the thousands of mines scattered over the area. A captured German engineer map later revealed that over 3,800 S-mines and antitank mines had been laid on the south-west approaches to Bitche, and flail tanks had to be called in to clear a narrow path through them.

The following day the 1st Battalion of the 398th Infantry braved heavy artillery fire to capture Fort Otterbiel, while the 2nd and 3rd Battalions and the 399th Infantry battled their way into Bitche itself. The town was cleared by nightfall and seventy-five prisoners taken, including the garrison commander; General Burress, commanding the 100th Division, was later made the first 'citizen of honour' in Bitche's history. The 100th then pushed on towards the Siegfried Line, leaving the 71st Division to assume control of the Bitche sector.

VI Corps, meanwhile, had begun its mission to clear northern Alsace and drive along the Rhine Valley. At 0100 on March 15th, four infantry divisions—the 42nd, 103rd, 36th and 3rd Algerian, extending from west to east in line abreast—struck silently across the Rothbach and Moder Rivers, supported by the 14th Armoured Division. Prisoners-of-war stated that the Allied attack had achieved total surprise, disrupting communications and throwing the German chain of command into confusion.

The 42nd Division drove into the enemy's mountain defences of the Low Vosges at 0645 on March 15th. All units moved along the ridges, deliberately avoiding the roads—which were heavily mined and blocked—and supplies were brought up by pack mule. They continued to advance north-eastwards on the 16th, pushing on through densely wooded terrain, and on the 18th they crossed the German border and reached the outer defences of the Siegfried Line. In three and a half days the division had traversed 16 miles of mountainous country.

To the right of the 42nd Division, the 103rd had also attacked at 0645 on the 15th, and had three battalions over the Rothbach River by 0800. Their 410th Infantry pushed on to capture Uttenhoffen, but had to abandon the town temporarily under a blanket of heavy German artillery fire. The 103rd Division crossed into Germany on March 18th and captured two intact bridges over the Lauter River at Bobenthal; these had been built by the Americans during the December campaign; and, although the Germans had prepared them for demolition, the speed of the Allied advance had prevented their destruction.

Training for the Seventh Army's spring
assault on the Siegfried Line, at
Sarreguemines, France, men of the 63rd
Division demolish a pillbox with grenades
and explosives.

Further east on VI Corps front, the 36th Division had been assigned the task of forcing the Wissembourg Gap and uncovering the Siegfried Line beyond it. The plan called for the 141st Infantry to thrust northward from Haguenau, while the 143rd advanced on Gunstett north-west of Haguenau Forest and the 142nd took Mertzwiller. The 142nd and 143rd both jumped off at 0100 on the 15th, the 143rd spearheading the advance into Bitschhoffen. The enemy had clearly planned to defend this town; the approaches were heavily mined and there were dug-in defences for machine-guns, mortar and artillery sites. However, the sheer momentum of the American drive carried the day and Bitschhoffen fell at 1045 that same morning. The next day, the 143rd organised a battalion of motorised infantry to race on to Soultz at top speed; it was stopped south of Eberbach by a blown bridge, but the Americans rapidly zeroed-in high velocity weapons and machine-guns to protect the river crossing site from heights nearby and engineers built a bridge overnight. On the 17th, the battalion crossed the river and swept on to take Dieffenbach with lightning speed.

The 142nd Infantry, meanwhile, had become involved in a fierce battle in the Haguenau Forest after crossing the Moder on footbridges. Almost as soon as they reached the further bank, they ran into a savage crossfire from bunkers and trenches among the trees. After a point-blank gunfight lasting half the day, the Americans got the upper hand and the surviving Germans began to fall back towards a new line on the Zintel River, and it was in this direction that the 142nd now turned the main weight of its assault. Before dawn on March 16th, five battalions of Allied artillery hurled 900 rounds across the Zintel in five minutes, and at 0430 two companies of the 142nd got across and engaged the Germans while engineers erected a Bailey Bridge to take supporting armour. The enemy positions were quickly overrun, the Americans taking 303 prisoners.

After taking Mertzwiller, the 142nd followed the 143rd's example and formed a fast motorised column. On March 19th they set off for Wissembourg, overwhelming a road-block and taking fifty more prisoners on the way. Wissembourg itself had been abandoned by the enemy, and there was no further contact until the 142nd crossed into German territory, when enemy artillery opened up on the town and the roads along the line of the American advance.

The 36th Division's 141st Infantry had crossed the Moder River in the early hours of March 15th. By first light they were well into the Haguenau Forest. Felled trees and mine clearance operations slowed the Regiment's progress, but within three days it had taken Surbourg and reached a position east of the line where the 142nd had been brought to a halt by artillery fire. At dusk on the 19th, the 141st sent out a two-company probe to see if there were enemy troops in the dragon's teeth defences and pillboxes of the Siegfried Line facing the regiment; there were. The two companies came under heavy fire from no fewer than fifteen well-concealed machine-guns and made a hasty withdrawal.

On the extreme right of VI Corps, the 3rd Algerian Infantry Division—reinforced by elements of the 5th French Armoured Division—had been given the task of taking Lauterbourg and securing crossings over the Lauter River. Against only minimal opposition, the Algerians pushed northward along the west bank of the Rhine as far as the frontier, crossing the Lauter on March 19th while the French armour occupied Schiebenhard and Lauterbourg. After that German resistance stiffened, but a French task force—Groupement Monsabert, commanded by the General of that name—drove on to occupy Berg. Night patrols penetrated as far as Neuburg, which was found to be flooded. By March 20th the French had made firm contact all along their front with the Siegfried defences.

Meanwhile, the American 14th Armoured Division, which was to spearhead a VI Corps breakthrough, passed through the 36th Division next to the French and advanced to points within sight of the German border. There was no opposition. On March 19th, elements of the division crossed the Lauter over a ford filled in by US engineers, and next day reached the Siegfried Line.

During the first five days of the Seventh Army's March offensive, VI Corps units on the right flank covered a greater distance than any other Allied formations. Moving more than 20 miles from the Moder River line near Haguenau across the German border, their line had run from west of Saarbrücken south-east through Haguenau; now it was being swung on a pivot near Saarbrücken to form a west-east line as the Seventh Army pushed all its divisions against the part of the German West Wall which formed a defence against penetration from the south. At the same time, XXI and XV Corps on the army's left flank were already starting to break their way through the Siegfried defences, while in the west more Seventh Army divisions raced across the Saar-Palatinate towards the Rhine.

The first days of the offensive had meant almost no progress in terms of distance for the divisions under XXI Corps, which were already at the Siegfried Line when the big push started. Although the corps had had the specific mission of capturing Saarbrücken and other towns as a preliminary to a drive north-eastwards to the Rhine, the penetration of the enemy's defences in this sector was a foot-by-foot business. In common with other Seventh Army formations, the Corps had opened its assault at 0100 on March 15th, with the 63rd Division probing the Siegfried defences and the

12th Armoured Division standing by to exploit any opening. On the left, the 70th Division and 101st Cavalry Group were to contain the enemy, patrol across the Sarre, and force a crossing if possible.

The 70th Division was delayed at the outset by German counter-attacks south of Saarbrücken. Then, at 1510 on D-Day, five battalions of American artillery opened up with a devastating twenty-minute barrage on the German positions in front of the town, repeating the process after a ten-minute lull. The gunners then shifted their fire to fresh positions 600 yards to the north, hitting the enemy with a third softening-up spell. While the barrage was still in progress, the 1st Battalion of the 274th Infantry, supported by two platoons of tanks and a platoon of tank destroyers, began to snake towards the fortifications in the area south of the city. But the terrain offered little cover, and the Germans had all approaches covered by interlocking fields of fire from pillboxes and bunkers; after several hundred yards the Americans were suffering too heavily to continue.

The next few days were marked by vigorous patrolling on the southern banks of the Sarre, while US artillery and tank destroyers hurled over 5,000 high explosive and armour-piercing shells at enemy gun batteries and bunkers. Then, on March 18th, word was received at XXI Corps HQ that the US Third Army had cut deep into the rear of the Saar region and had reached St Wendel; since the Germans would not dare risk being cut off on the wrong side of the Rhine, they were tactically bound to withdraw, opening the way for the 70th Division to thrust on against weakening opposition. On the 19th, the 70th was therefore ordered to establish a bridgehead over the Sarre and be prepared either to exploit the situation northwards or reduce Saarbrücken. For the river crossing the Americans concentrated all their available fire power in the area; the 433rd Anti-Aircraft Battalion, for example, used its 40mm cannon and M51 a/a machine-guns as ground support weapons to help neutralise the remaining pillboxes on the other bank. All visible enemy positions were bombarded. The Germans retaliated with intense fire, but it was not long before air reconnaissance showed long columns of enemy troops and civilians withdrawing to the east, churning up clouds of dust on the roads that led deep into the Saar. This time the Germans did not neglect to blow up the bridges in their wake, but nothing could stop the Allied advance now.

At 2230 on March 19th, a patrol from the 176th Infantry crossed the Sarre near Hostenbach on the extreme west flank of the Seventh Army. They found no enemy opposition, but a lot of mines had been laid on the opposite bank and a path had to be cleared by an anti-mine platoon before the main body of the 70th Division could cross. On the 20th, advance

Above: A Bangalore torpedo opens up a pathway through the wire as men of the Seventh Army attack a simulated pillbox during training for the assault on the Siegfried Line.

Below: Leaving the roads, Seventh Army troops enter mountainous country around Pit Wingen, France, in a right wing thrust towards the Rhine during March, 1945.

elements of the 70th moved forward in an eerie silence past deserted enemy bunkers and pillboxes from which, only a matter of hours earlier, a murderous fire had spat out across the river. At noon, the 276th Infantry began an advance on Saarbrücken itself, and the town was occupied at nightfall without the loss of a single American soldier.

East of the city, the 63rd Division had secured good positions for an assault on the Siegfried Line. As its attack developed on March 15th-17th, the Division had to withstand several counter-punches by enemy tanks and infantry, but these were beaten off.

The overall situation in the Saar-Palatinate by March 17th could have given the Germans but cold comfort; the US Third Army's drive south from the Moselle was rapidly rolling up Army Group G. The German First Army forces facing the US Seventh Army betrayed their lack of defence in depth by withdrawing into the shell of the Siegfried Line with the evident object of maintaining a secure left flank and preserving potential crossing sites over the Rhine. As the Sixth Army Group's weekly Intelligence Bulletin put it on March 17th: "There is no doubt that the enemy will eventually be forced across the Rhine if only because of his inability to reinforce present positions. General Hausser, Commander of Army Group G, can decide only how many Germans he wishes to leave in our hands west of the Rhine."

Hausser was well aware of the threat posed to his forces by the Allied crossing of the lower Moselle. Since there were no real defences in the Hunsrück sector, a thrust by the Third US Army into the Rhine Plain via Bad Kreuznach was a strong possibility, and in that event the German position in the Saar-Palatinate would be completely untenable. Hausser therefore wanted to withdraw his forces as early as possible in order to undertake the defence of the Rhine in full combat strength, but because of economic considerations—such as the vital coalfields near Saarbrücken—he was ordered to hold the area for as long as possible.

By March 16th, Third Army G-2 was of the opinion that the Allied sweep across the enemy rear in the Palatinate triangle was creating a situation similar to that in the Falaise Pocket in north-western France. They were threatened with encirclement. Moreover it seemed probable that, with the German lines of communication in a turmoil as a result of the Allied advances, the enemy did not have a clear picture of this danger to themselves. The Germans had some 36,000 combat effectives in the Palatinate triangle—the equivalent of about 40 per cent of their front-line forces in the west—and the bulk of them would have to be extricated if there was to be any hope of a successful stand east of the Rhine.

At their March 17th meeting in Lunéville, Eisenhower had asked Patch where and when he expected the Seventh Army to break through the Siegfried Line. Patch replied that he could not say when, but he would expect it to be in the XV Corps zone, perhaps to the right of XXI Corps before the 63rd Division. His forecast was accurate; it was just three days later, on March 20th, that penetration was achieved, with three divisions—the 63rd, 45th and 3rd—each succeeding in breaching the German defences.

It was no mean achievement. On the Seventh Army front the main Siegfried defences consisted of a belt of dragon's teeth, three rows of concrete pyramids about 3ft high straddling the countryside in a continuous staggered zig-zag line; behind them were two antitank ditches each 8ft deep and 12ft wide. On every knoll and covering every path through the woods, there were concrete pillboxes, so situated that each one was covered by fire from one or more of the others. Each group of between three and six pillboxes was commanded from a central control bunker. The line itself was some 500 yards deep, though well-camouflaged pillboxes in secondary positions dotted knolls and rises for miles back. Most of the fortifications were covered with earth and vegetation, and the entrances to the tunnels giving access to the pillboxes were usually as much as 150 yards to the rear.

A study of aerial photographs suggested that the best spot to effect a penetration of the dragon's teeth was 50 yards east of the main north-south road to the north of Ensheim. The road here had been blocked by the demolition of a timber bridge over an antitank ditch immediately to the rear of the teeth. In the early hours of March 18th, after several attempts, a company of the 263rd Combat Engineer Battalion reached the dragon's teeth just north of Ensheim; the advance was made over flat, open terrain swept by German machine-gun fire, but the engineers weathered the storm and at 0130 they blasted a gap in the teeth with 1,500lb of TNT. A few hours later a task force of five tanks, four destroyers, a platoon of engineers and a tank dozer moved up to the gap. While the armour covered them, the engineers cleared a path through the minefield, working on their knees with streams of bullets from fixed-angle enemy machine-guns crackling just a few inches over their heads.

Meanwhile, similar operations were in progress in the eastern sector of the 63rd Division's area north of Ommersheim. At 2200 on the 18th, after repeated attempts under heavy fire, a gap was blown in the dragon's teeth here also.

During the next twenty-four hours, the division stepped up its pressure on the Siegfried Line, systematically eliminating one pillbox after another. On March 19th, no fewer than forty-eight pillboxes were knocked out, and

Above: Dragon's teeth tank obstacles, anti-tank ditches, pillboxes and other defences 500 yards deep met Seventh Army troops as they approached the Siegfried Line In March, 1945.

Below: Infantrymen of the 63rd Division climb the dragon's teeth obstacles in front of the Siegfried Line near Würzbach. In the Seventh Army's eastern sector, the defences were first breeched by the 63rd Division.

the following morning the 63rd penetrated the line completely. The first to break through was the 254th Infantry, which reached Ober-Würzbach north of Ommersheim, and shortly afterwards the 255th Infantry pierced it near Nieder-Würzbach. Every pillbox captured intact was blown up by the American engineers to prevent possible reoccupation by the Germans.

Once the 63rd Division had broken through, the Americans moved on rapidly into Hassel and St Ingbert. After that they fanned out to right and left, with elements proceeding to Homburg to join XV Corps; and a second force, Task Force Harris, pushing on to seize and hold objectives around Neunkirchen where they made contact with XX Corps of the Third Army. Meanwhile, the 70th Division was also pushing north to meet up with Third Army units.

On March 21st, less than a week after the start of the offensive, Task Force Harris—spearheading the assault of the 63rd Division—cleared Neunkirchen, rounding up 1,000 German prisoners and forced labourers. All organised resistance here quickly collapsed. While divisional elements were mopping up, 6th Armoured Division units surged eastwards to reach Rhein-Dürkheim on the west bank of the Rhine by noon. Patrols entered Worms to meet elements of the Third Army. Next day, XXI Corps assumed command of the 71st and 100th Divisions around Bitche, and these two advanced north through the broken Siegfried defences before turning east towards the Rhine. Their motorised columns broke through only light opposition to reach the Landau-Neustadt-Germersheim area.

On the XV Corps front, the 45th Division had also been making spectacular headway through the Siegfried defences along the Blies River Valley. At 1400 on March 18th, following a thirty-minute artillery barrage, the 157th Infantry jumped off and attacked the enemy line with armoured support. The tanks rolled up as far as the dragon's teeth would permit and opened fire on the pillboxes, while infantry and demolition squads blew a path through the obstacles. Nine pillboxes were destroyed and the jubilant Americans rode through the line clinging to their tanks.

On March 19th, the 45th captured or destroyed eighty-six pillboxes and bunkers and captured three key towns. So rapid was the American advance that in one place they seized a German military switchboard which was still in full operation—a real windfall; because two Intelligence officers, sent along by the S-2 of the 157th Infantry to listen in to conversations, overheard an SS captain issuing orders for a withdrawal to Landstuhl. This information was duly relayed to XII TAF and a squadron of night intruders took off to search for enemy movements towards that town. It was not long before they located a convoy of enemy vehicles, three abreast and extending for several miles; for the next hour American ground forces were treated to the spectacle of a lurid glow on the horizon and the crump of bombs as the aircraft did their stuff.

At dawn on March 21st—the first day of spring—the 45th Division renewed its attack, brushing aside a small delaying force and setting off in hot pursuit of the enemy. The Americans caught long columns of troops and vehicles packing the exit roads from their sector; by nightfall the enemy forces were totally disorganised, with small groups of German soldiers roaming over the countryside in an effort to escape from the trap. The German lines of communication were in such a desperate state of disruption, and the American advance so bewilderingly fast, that enemy troops were still trying to withdraw through Homburg on March 21st—twenty-four hours after the town had been taken by the 179th US Infantry.

The men of the 157th Infantry, moving forward east of Homburg, found new heart from the fact that their advance was virtually unopposed. France lay behind them now, and there were signs everywhere that the Allied blows were inflicting crippling hurt on the enemy. They passed hundreds of German prisoners, on their way to the rear for processing, some riding in trucks but most straggling along dispiritedly, staring with a kind of blank amazement at the well-fed, well-equipped American troops, at the flood of trucks and armour roaring past them on its way to the Rhine.

The 45th Division continued to mop up the area throughout March 21st, taking a total of 2,055 prisoners and eventually joining up with elements of the Third Army, attacking south-eastwards across the German rear. The 179th Infantry, in the wake of the 6th Armoured Division, reached high ground north of Kaiserslautern and continued to the Rhine the next day.

Further east, on the right flank of the 45th Division, the 3rd Division also broke through the Siegfried Line south-east of Zweibrücken on March 18th, the infantry jumping-off at 0545 in the wake of a 25,000-round artillery bombardment. The 7th Infantry Regiment made slow progress and the 15th was subjected to fierce counter-attacks as it tried to penetrate the dragon's teeth; there were also mines at every step and all bridges had been blown. Nevertheless, by noon the following day the Americans had fought their way through to a point 1 mile south-east of Contwig. The infantry received excellent air support from XII TAF and artillery throughout; tanks used 76mm ammunition to penetrate the larger pillboxes, hitting the same points alternately with high-explosive and armour-piercing shells. Bitter fighting went on all night, but the next morning the Americans broke through and entered Zweibrücken. Captured Germans stated that they had little confidence in the much-vaunted Siegfried Line; seasoned veterans did not like the way its defences were laid out. Although troops manning the pillboxes were supposed to fight for as long as possible from trenches around the emplacements, most of them retreated inside as soon as the Americans were sighted. Conditions in the boxes were claustrophobic, and many crews were seized by panic; some surrendered when they mistook the bursts of white phosphorous shells for gas.

In the afternoon of March 20th, the 6th Armoured Division passed through the 3rd Division to exploit the situation towards the Rhine. As the momentum of the drive increased, the tally of captured enemy material became tremendous; all American units overran large quantities of guns, ammunition, explosives and other equipment. By midnight on March 23rd, the 3rd Division had assembled on the edge of the Rhine Plain south of Worms, and XV Corps, with the 45th and 3rd Divisions on the east bank of the river, began to prepare for a crossing once its drive had been completed on all fronts.

Down on the right flank of the Seventh Army, the Germans held on to their defences as long as possible to prevent their escape route across the Rhine from being sealed. VI Corps, with the 42nd, 103rd and 36th Divisions, and Groupement Monsabert with the 14th Armoured Division in support, continued the drive they had begun on March 15th, although progress was slow. The 42nd Division was trying to push along the ridge of the Hardt Mountains when it was halted by murderous artillery fire; it was only able to continue after a devastating Allied air strike and artillery barrage at dusk on March 21st, and by the time the Americans penetrated the Siegfried defences in this sector the enemy had successfully withdrawn.

Meanwhile, the 103rd Division was engaged in clearing the eastern foothills of the Hardt Mountains. Here the division was involved in a fierce battle for the best part of thirty-six hours before air strikes and artillery tipped the scales in their favour and the enemy began to show signs of disorganisation. Prisoners disclosed that some units had been told to fight a delaying action and then retire to the Rhine, while others had been ordered to fight to the last man. At nightfall on the 22nd, the 103rd took 1,321 prisoners in a mass surrender, and nearly twice as many were rounded up the following day.

Over on the 36th Division front, the Americans were also involved in heavy fighting against the Siegfried defences in the Wissembourg Gap. The division had driven a wedge into the enemy lines on March 20th, and after that its operations became a straightforward slugging match against the pillboxes in its path. It took the 36th the whole of March 21st to eliminate eight strongpoints; the crews of all but two closed their hatches and refused to listen to American surrender demands, shouted to them through air vents. The Americans immediately saturated the obstinate pillboxes with hand grenades, bazooka rockets and burning gasoline, but even this had no effect and there was no surrender until engineer teams detonated special explosive charges known as beehives on roofs and at apertures and doorways. After this initial delay, progress was a good deal faster, and by the end of the next day the division had destroyed some 200 pillboxes.

By March 25th, all three corps of the Seventh Army, co-operating with the Third Army's drive from the north, had completely overrun the triangle of the Saar-Palatinate. Allied troops pushing on through the area found chaotic conditions prevailing in most cities. In Zweibrücken, the entire business district had been razed to the ground, while the rest of the town was damaged to a more or less severe extent. Only 5,000 out of a normal population of 37,000 still remained, hiding in basements and cellars. There was no water or sanitation and parts of the town still burned. Rubble and craters scarred and pitted the streets. All officials had long since fled. Thousands of released Allied prisoners and forced workers roamed the place aimlessly, as though terrified of their new-found freedom.

Homburg was even worse. Dead horses and human corpses littered the business district, where fires still raged. Wholesale looting added to the general chaos, and there were several minor riots. In Bad Dürkheim, which had been a wine and spirit centre, the problem of drunkenness was thrown in as well. Just before being occupied, the town had been subjected to a very heavy air attack, and an estimated 400 civilians still lay buried beneath the rubble. Dead horses were strewn over the roads leading out of town and, like its neighbours, the place was overflowing with ex-prisoners and displaced persons, all of whom had to be fed and temporarily housed by the Seventh Army.

The rapid collapse of the German defences in the Palatinate had been attributable in the first instance to the complete tactical surprise achieved by the Americans. After that, air support had played a leading part in blasting a path for the ground forces. As the 45th Division Commander said in a message to General Barcus, commanding XII TAF: "It is difficult to describe the devastation which . . . fighter-bombers have wrought. So intense has been the attack that scarcely a man-made thing exists in their wake; it is even difficult to find buildings suitable for CPs: this is the scorched earth . . . The ground forces have come to think of the destruction of towns and the softening up of strongpoints by bombing as a necessary part of any attack."

The German First and Seventh Armies had been defeated before, but never quite so badly as in the debacle of the Saar-Palatinate. Prisoners numbered 100,000. No count was made of enemy losses in material, but estimates suggested that most of the enemy's artillery had been left west of the Rhine. Before the offensive, these two German armies had controlled twenty-three divisions; in less than two weeks, they had lost 75 per cent of their combat effectives.

Not unnaturally, it was General Paul Hausser who served as Hitler's scapegoat. Questioned later by the Allies on his defeat, he told them that he blamed the disaster entirely on the policy that required some of his finest units to hold on to the last man. He knew how vulnerable his position was, but claimed that his suggestion of shortening the line had been rejected outright. When Allied forces secured the vital Ludendorff railway bridge at Remagen, he again recommended withdrawal to the Rhine, and again he was refused. Once more, Hitler had waited too long. Now the Allied armies were massing across the Rhine, and they would not be on the other side for long.

XI

The Siegfried Line was broken, and now the Rhine represented the last real obstacle to the Allied advance into the heart of Germany. Plans to cross the river were well in hand even before the Saar-Palatinate had been cleared; the Allies did not intend to waste time in exploiting the impetus of their success.

Exactly a week after launching the Saar offensive, the Seventh Army ordered its 3rd and 45th Divisions to halt the bulk of their forces west of the line Alzey-Grünstadt-Wachenheim and reconnoitre the river for crossing sites. To prepare for the actual operation, XV Corps was ordered on March 23rd to relieve all Third Army units holding the west bank of the Rhine in its zone; this task was carried out by reserve regiments of the 3rd and 45th.

Next day, boat lists were revised and vehicle priority lists prepared for the crossing. Since the assault craft were not yet ready, troops carried out training in mock 'boats' outlined on the ground with tape. As the motorised columns of the two engineer river crossing groups—each about 35 miles long—rumbled towards the Worms region, the infantry divisions edged forward towards the Rhine, approaching the west bank under cover of darkness.

The 45th Division had a zone on the left flank of XV Corps, and on March 23rd its 157th Regiment was assigned to patrol the east bank in this sector. The 179th and 180th, the assault regiments, remained further to the rear and went on with their training. To the south, the 3rd Division employed its 15th Regiment for patrolling, while the 7th and 30th prepared for the crossing.

The power of the Rhine was harnessed by nine dams on the river and its tributaries, and the Allied engineers had to consider the possibility that the enemy might release the waters pent upstream by these controls to interfere with the crossings. Opening the weir gates or destroying the dams would loose 6,240 million cubic feet of water, a powerful last-ditch weapon which would sweep bridges from the Rhine and inundate the Swiss, French and German lowlands. To forestall such a move, the Allied air forces had attacked some of the dams during previous months; on October 7th, 1944, for example, the Kembs dam on the upper Rhine had been breached by 12,000lb 'Tallboy' bombs dropped by the Lancasters of No 617 Squadron RAF, but most of the others were still intact and represented a serious threat. Operation of the weir gates was subject to a joint agreement between Germany and Switzerland, so diplomatic steps were taken to see that the Swiss Government took all necessary action to safeguard the weirs on the Rhine between Lake Constance and Basel.

The initial crossing of the river was to be made by high-speed storm boats, and 72 two-man crews from each battalion were trained in their operation on the fast-flowing Rhône River.

The XV Corps had short final notice for the attack. Its field order for the assault were issued at midnight on March 24th-25th, but at that time no D-Day had been assigned. In fact it was to be only twenty-six hours away, as the troops were finally told on March 25th. The plan called for the 45th Division to force a crossing north of Worms, while the 3rd Division was to cross further south. The initial object was to cut the Gernsheim-Mannheim railway line, following which both divisions were to attack eastward into the Odenwald mountains. Follow-up troops were to cross as soon as practicable; these were the 63rd and 44th Divisions.

By March 25th, the Seventh Army zone west of the Rhine had been cleared of all enemy except for a small pocket in the south-west part of Ludwigshaffen, which was being mopped up by XXI Corps. On the night of March 24th/25th, the assault elements of XV Corps moved up to the Rhine and assembled two or three miles from the river. Patrols had previously carried out extensive reconnaissance on the west bank, while liaison aircraft had been used to give commanders of all echelons a first hand view of the river and the terrain over which they were to attack.

From personal observation, maps and G-2 information, it was established that at the crossing areas the Rhine was about 1,000ft wide and 17ft deep, flowing swiftly between revetted banks. The country on both sides was flat and sparsely wooded, so men and equipment had to be concentrated under cover of darkness. Parallel with the Rhine in the assault area ran the Odenwald Mountains, some 8 miles east of the river. They were roughly 40 miles long and 32 miles in depth, rising sharply out of the Rhine Plain. Any exploitation in the Worms area, although not initially hampered by these mountains, might be seriously threatened if the enemy chose to make a stand there in an attempt to contain the Rhine bridgehead.

It was impossible to make an accurate assessment of enemy strength opposing XV Corps, and at that time it was quite probable that even the Germans themselves did not know the full extent of their forces on the east bank. Remnants of twenty-two divisions were believed to have escaped across the river in XV Corps zone, and the Americans thought that the average enemy strength would not be more than fifty men per river-front kilometre. Based on experience at Strasbourg and Colmar, they also thought that the enemy would have no large guns permanently emplaced east of the Rhine, and that the only artillery opposition might be expected to come from divisional and corps weapons.

To oppose the bridgehead, the Germans were expected to make a determined effort to resist the actual crossing—but this was thought to present less of a hazard than the current. A first-hand study of the far shore was carried out by the commander of the 1st Battalion, 180th Infantry, who took three men and paddled across the Rhine in a rubber boat at midnight on March 24th/25th. No one spotted the little craft as it bobbed eastwards to land in the Altrhein Canal. There, the four men reconnoitred the area for half an hour but found no mines, wire or emplacements.

The date and time of the Rhine crossing was fixed at 0230 on March 26th. Under a moon periodically obscured by cloud, engineers began to prepare the approaches to the river banks. On the other side the enemy, jumpy as a result of two feints made across the river earlier in the evening of the 25th, heard activity in the 3rd Division's zone and opened fire with mortars and artillery.

At 0152, the Allied guns opened up. All weapons in the 3rd Division sector, where surprise had already been lost, saturated the far shore with 12,000 rounds directed at known defensive positions and gun emplacements. To the north, the guns of the 45th Division stayed temporarily silent to preserve an element of secrecy. While the artillery preparation continued, the first wave of the five taking part in the assault moved up to the river from the assembly areas, carrying their storm boats or pulling them on handcarts. At 0225 a sudden, eerie silence descended on the Rhine as the thirty-minute Allied artillery barrage ceased. Five minutes later, the hush was once more broken by the throbbing of 100 50hp engines as the first wave of storm boats headed out across the river. The crossing took less than thirty seconds, and at 0231 all four regiments were establishing a bridgehead on the east bank along a 9-mile stretch of the river.

On the left of the assault, the 179th Regiment of the 45th Division crossed near Hamm and the 180th near Rheim Dürkeim. Both regiments encountered 88mm, small-arms and mortar fire during the crossing, and casualties began to mount as they hit the far shore. The second assault wave

Above: The Seventh Army crossed the Rhine on 26th March, 1945. Here infantrymen of the 3rd Division and a tank destroyer use the heavy pontoon bridge constructed on D-Day by the 540th Engineer Combat Group.

Below: An overturned car-load of bazookas in the railway yard at Worms, blasted by Allied bombers.

fared even worse, losing nearly half its craft to the enemy artillery. Many troops were swept away and drowned in the fast-flowing current.

Once on the east bank, the two assault battalions of each regiment fought hard to establish a foothold and then began to fan out. All assault elements of the 179th were over and pushing inland by 0315 in the face of deteriorating enemy resistance. The garrisons of several small towns in the bridgehead offered strong opposition, but they were quickly outflanked and subdued at the Americans' leisure. By 0800, the 45th Division had reached the railway line and begun its drive to the Corps's bridgehead line—the autobahn in the eastern edge of the woods. The 179th had contacted the Third Army on the left, while the 180th called in two squadrons of aircraft to soften resistance in the town of Gross Hausen. The 45th Division reached its Corps line along the whole front by 1720 on D-Day.

The 3rd Division's crossing of the Rhine, on the right of the Seventh Army, was accomplished against only light opposition; this, however, increased as the Americans pushed inland. The 30th Infantry, on the division's left, encountered machine-gun and mortar fire as they went over near Worms, but both battalions were deploying on the east bank by 0300. Advancing slowly, the 2nd Battalion on the left attacked Bürstadt, where they ran into stiff resistance from automatics, mortars and tank guns. A fierce battle developed before the enemy was finally overwhelmed. The 3rd Battalion also had to fight hard for the town of Lampertheim, which fell at 1300. To the right of the 30th Regiment, the 7th Infantry crossed the river north of Mannheim, and by 0340 both battalions were firmly established and driving towards the railway line.

Meanwhile, enemy fire was still coming from machine-guns and 88mm antiaircraft weapons located on an island in the centre of the river, midway between the 3rd Division's two bridgeheads. The island was eventually cleared at noon by the 3rd Battalion of the 15th Infantry, while the rest of the regiment attacked towards the autobahn through the Loracher Wald.

As the assault teams drove steadily eastwards, the back-up forces went over the river on schedule, despite a withering artillery fire the Germans had by this time ranged on the crossing sites. All fourteen DD tanks assigned to the 45th Division crossed safely, and so did ten of the fourteen assigned to the 3rd Division. Three of the others were sunk by enemy in the 7th Infantry's sector, and the fourth was destroyed as it churned up the far bank. All the DD tanks were relieved on D-plus-1 by armour which had crossed on bridges and rafts.

As soon as the small-arms fire ceased to harass the crossing sites, engineers in both assault areas began to build floating bridges, still under artillery and mortar fire. Behind the 3rd Division, the 540th Engineer Combat Group threw up two heavy pontoon rafts and two infantry support rafts. By the end of D-Day itself, the Group had completed a 948ft treadway bridge and a 1,040ft heavy pontoon bridge. The latter was built in only 9 hours 12 minutes. Two heavy pontoon rafts and two infantry support rafts operated by the 40th Engineer Combat Group backed up the 45th Division's drive, and by the end of D-Day a heavy pontoon bridge and a floating treadway bridge were also nearing completion in this Division's sector. The 1st Field Artillery Battalion crossed the river three and a half hours after H-Hour, and all artillery supporting the four assault regiments crossed six hours later. During the first twenty-four hours of raft operation, 1,000 vehicles were transported. Evacuation of casualties was carried out by DUKW and ferry, as all bridges were 'one way only'.

By March 27th, D-plus-1, it was believed that the enemy was making a break for the rear to set-up a line of defence along the Main River. Both the 45th and 3rd Divisions mounted troops on tanks, tank destroyers and trucks to sweep into the Odenwald and overtake the Germans, supplementing their drive with enemy vehicles captured the previous day. The 45th Division raced on with three regiments in line abreast, while on the left the 157th pushed forward 16 miles and sent out patrols to the River Main. By this time, the Americans considered their Rhine bridgehead to be secure, although the Seventh Army line on the east bank had not been reached at all points. To oppose the expansion of the bridgehead, the Germans had only a miscellany of stop-gap units; the burden of defence fell on forty antiaircraft units, which used their guns as ground support weapons and then fought on as infantry when the guns were destroyed. Maintenance and supply units were also committed in support of the German combat divisions, which were unable to field more than 15 per cent of their effectives during this phase. It was now clear that the enemy regarded the Ruhr as more valuable than the Frankfurt Mannheim area facing the Seventh Army, and did not intend to divert troops there from the northern front.

By the time the Seventh Army had secured itself east of the Rhine, it had no less than ten infantry divisions under its control, three armoured divisions and two cavalry groups, all preparing for a massive offensive in April. The Germans were now in a serious dilemma. They had no more than 6,000 combat effectives on the Seventh Army front, and so it seemed impossible to prevent an American drive north-eastward from the bridgehead without diverting troops from the Ruhr—yet failure to stop such a drive would further endanger the Ruhr and probably lead to the splitting of northern and southern Germany.

Facing the Seventh Army's advance rose the heavily wooded slopes of the Odenwald Hills. The enemy could expect an attack either north-eastward around the Odenwald towards Frankfurt, the Main Valley and the Fulda Pass, eastward through the Odenwald to the Main plains, or south-eastward through the 30-mile-wide valley between the Odenwald and the Black Forest. On March 25th, G-2 issued a study of the German national redoubt or 'last stand' area, estimating that they would continue to defend the ground they now held, give ground or counter-attack when necessary, and finally—when forced to do so—abandon northern Germany and the Ruhr and retire to the Alps for a final stand. The enemy must realise, reported G-2, that the Alps region was the only real defensive area left; troops from the eastern, Italian and western fronts might conceivably find a way back to this, the most rugged terrain in Europe. The enemy's communications network, too, favoured a stand in the Alps; the road and rail nets of southern Germany ran generally north and south, while a series of autobahns led south to the Alps from Frankfurt, Heilbronn and Nuremberg. It was possible that a quarter of a million Nazis might muster there to fight to the last under the direction of Hitler or Himmler.

At the end of March, SHAEF stated in Paris that it expected Sixth Army Group to launch a thrust on its right towards southern Germany, but only after the Ruhr pocket had been reduced and the enemy armies in western and central Germany had been defeated. In the beginning, when the isolation of the Ruhr was still the main objective, the Seventh Army was to make its main effort on the left, to relieve elements of the Third Army south of the Main, and drive north-east to protect their right flank as far north as the Höhe Rhon.

After the Americans had secured their Rhine bridgehead, XV Corps jumped off again on March 28th. The 3rd and 45th Divisions headed for the Höhe Rhon hills, while the 12th Armoured Division pushed ahead to clear the Odenwald. The 44th struck south along the Rhine towards Mannheim and Heidelberg. By March 30th, XV Corps had cleared most of the Odenwald Mountains.

On March 28th, the 44th Division reached Mannheim, and the city was occupied almost without a hitch. The acting-Burgomeister called a US command post from a civilian telephone that afternoon, saying that all German troops had left the city, which would surrender at once. Negotiations were opened, and a time and place fixed for a meeting. When the assistant-commander of the 44th Division arrived on time at the designated spot, however, he was greeted by a mortar barrage. It turned out that an agitated Burgomeister had called the command post a few minutes earlier to warn the Americans that the German troops had not departed after all, and would not allow him to surrender. The troops finally left during the night, and Mannheim surrendered the following morning.

Meanwhile, the 3rd and 45th Divisions struck out rapidly for the River Main, which they reached and crossed. Although the actual crossing was easy, the 157th, 179th and 180th Regiments all encountered strong opposition on the other side before breaking through and continuing their push. The 157th met serious resistance at Aschaffenburg, where the enemy held out for six days. The commander of the 157th had tried to by-pass the town and take it in a pincer movement, but this plan was temporarily frustrated by bitter resistance in a suburb of Schweinheim. A frontal attack had to be carried out, with fierce house-to-house fighting made all the more difficult by the fact that enemy civilians were taking part in the battle. German reinforcements also arrived, many of them fanatical youths of 16 and 17 who refused to surrender and had to be annihilated.

Against this kind of opposition, the regiment punched into Aschaffenburg yard by yard, clearing the suburbs on March 30th without bayonet and hand grenade and outflanking the town on April 1st. Air strikes pounded the area hard, and, backed by intense artillery support, the two battalions of the 157th continued their grim, bloody drive in from the south. The defenders still had a lot of ammunition, and on March 31st they dropped some 1,500 mortar rounds in the path of the advancing Americans, inching forward over piles of rubble while 155mm shells exploded ahead of them. The bitter fight went on for another two days, until 0700 on April 3rd. During the latter stages the German commander hanged several of his own soldiers and civilians for advocating surrender.

The time was now ripe for an armoured thrust towards the Höhe Rhon mass, and the 14th Armoured Division—newly attached to XV Corps—sped on towards Neustadt through the lines of the 3rd and 45th Divisions. By April 9th, the Americans had reached the Höhe Rhon, and XV Corps now stood ready for an assault on Nuremberg. On the right, XXI Corps met their first serious opposition at Würzburg, a large, populous and much-bombed city on the north-east bank of the Main. To take it, an initial crossing of the river was made by elements of the 2nd Battalion, 222nd Infantry, which established a bridgehead in the town and extended it methodically. Once again, civilians joined German troops in defending their home town, retreating into the sewers and often appearing in the Americans's rear. Meanwhile, two bridges had been thrown across the Main and supporting armour of the 42nd Division rumbled across to hasten the end of the battle. The final spasm of resistance erupted in the form of a 200-man counter-attack, launched from the north of the city on

157

the morning of April 5th. It got to within 100 yards of the northern bridge before it was shrivelled up by the 232nd Regiment. The town of Würzburg fell later that day, after the last defenders had been killed or captured. There was no formal surrender.

The 42nd Division, supported by Combat Command A of the 12th Armoured Division, now swung towards the ball-bearing manufacturing centre of Schweinfurt, nestling in a bend of the River Main. Since the town had been a frequent target for Allied bombers, it was still strongly defended by antiaircraft guns, which could easily be adapted for use against ground targets. Every small town and village on the road to Schweinfurt was fortified, every hill and wood occupied by the enemy for as long as possible, often by fanatical Nazi youths. On April 11th, as bombers and artillery softened up Schweinfurt, the 42nd Division seized the high ground overlooking the town and launched their final attack next day. Surprisingly, resistance melted away rapidly among the shattered streets, and by nightfall Schweinfurt was in American hands.

While XV and XXI Corps were travelling north-eastwards, VI Corps was moving south-east at right-angles through the valley between the Odenwald and Black Forest. On the extreme right of the Seventh Army, the French crossed the Rhine near Speyer and plunged into the Black Forest, while VI Corps went over the river near Mannheim on March 31st. On April 1st, the 10th Armoured and 63rd Divisions joined the 100th Infantry in a drive on Heidelberg, which surrendered without a struggle. The first real opposition was encountered by Combat Command B of the 10th Armoured, which—driving south along the Rhine with the 399th Regiment of the 100th—was counter-attacked by enemy armour and infantry near Bruchsal. The American impetus could not be checked, however, and they took 300 prisoners in the action.

The rapid advance on the VI Corps front came to a sudden end on April 4th. The enemy reformed and built up a formidable crescent-shaped defensive line running from Heilbronn, along the River Neckar, and then along the Jagst. It was no mean achievement, considering the shattered condition of their combat units and the diminished power of both artillery and Luftwaffe. The Germans, however, were still unable to co-ordinate their forces to establish a real defensive line along the whole Seventh Army front, and their Nineteenth Army in the Siegfried Line and Black Forest—with an estimated 10,500 combat effectiveness—was in danger of being outflanked. The German Seventh Army was likewise falling back in confusion before the American Third Army and the XV Corps of the US Seventh; its combat strength was estimated to be only 4,000 men. Facing the VI and XXI Corps was the German First Army with about 7,500 troops.

Above: The ruins of Worms after Allied bombing.

Below: Infantrymen of the 3rd Division in another search for snipers in the rubble of Nuremberg, shrine of the Nazi movement, after the Seventh Army's capture of the city in April, 1945.

The enemy therefore had to improvise desperately. Every source was combed for men; training camps, barrage balloon detachments, maintenance units, horse pack companies, air signals regiments, labour battalions and the Volksturm, the German Home Guard. These men were assigned to organised divisions or formed into battle groups, which were given temporary missions and then disbanded. Besides all these, the Germans formed three new divisions, named Alpen, Donau and Bayern; these were in fact little more than large battle groups given names for reasons of morale. It was with such makeshift forces that the enemy formed its defensive crescent on the Jagst and Neckar.

VI Corps had not expected to be delayed on these two rivers, and on April 3rd orders went out for the 10th Armoured and 100th Divisions to seize Heilbronn and move east. The 3rd Battalion of the 398th Regiment crossed the Neckar in assault boats before dawn on April 4th, with the factory district of Heilbronn as their objective, and at first it seemed that they had taken the enemy by surprise. Then, at 0900, the Germans launched a strong counter-attack and the 3rd Battalion was hurled back, suffering heavy casualties. Two platoons were cut off and captured, and the Americans driven 1,000 yards back beyond the river.

A second bridgehead was established shortly afterwards by the 100th Division, with the 2nd Battalion of the 397th Infantry crossing the river further to the south. Here, too, the Americans suffered heavy losses, mainly at the hands of the Hitler Jugend. On the morning of the 5th, a company of HJ—most of them aged between fourteen and seventeen— broke under a fierce American mortar barrage and came running out of the factory district to surrender, screaming hysterically. Many of them never reached the American lines; they were mown down by their own officers.

On April 5th, the 3rd Battalion of the 397th also crossed the river; and, while their comrades of the 398th held on in the north, the two battalions of the 397th managed to advance 1,500 yards in three days. The Americans, however, had no direct heavy fire support and no armour. Enemy artillery from the hills had prevented the building of a bridge over the river and knocked out a ferry, and DD tanks had been unable to negotiate the river banks. The enemy had consequently been able to regroup after each American attack.

While the battle raged, the 1st Battalion of the 397th crossed the Neckar 2 miles to the south and drove towards the centre of Heilbronn. The Germans resisted furiously, supporting their counter-attacks with four Tiger tanks—two of which were knocked out by air strikes on April 6th. The strength of the enemy force opposing the 100th Division was never less than 1,000 men, and it was backed by accurate artillery; on April 7th,

American engineers had almost completed a treadway bridge over the river at the southern bridgehead when enemy shellfire destroyed it.

The supporting operation by the 10th Armoured Division fared better at first. Two days after leaving the 100th near Heilbronn, Combat Command A drove 30 miles south-east to Crailsheim, which it entered on April 7th. Then a strong enemy force struck at their main supply route as well as at the town itself. As Combat Command R also advanced on Crailsheim, it too was attacked by enemy groups in the woods, firing Panzerfaust antitank rockets, and by occasional German aircraft. On April 8th, the supply corridor to Combat Command A was closed by the Germans, but the next day Combat Command B cleared minefields and road-blocks to thrust on towards the town, flushing the woods of opposition as they went.

That night the route—although still open—was under continual threat of ambush, so supplies were airlifted by 60 C-47s, which landed on Crailsheim's captured airfield under fighter cover. On the return flight, they carried out wounded. A second mission was flown the following day, but by that time the ground supply route had been firmly secured. During this period, the Americans were engaged in a fierce fight with 500 SS troops, who penetrated Crailsheim early on April 8th. On the 9th, 600 more Waffen SS attacked the town, which was subsequently evacuated by the Americans.

All along the front, it was a question of slow progress in the teeth of fierce and often fanatical resistance. The experience of the 63rd and 100th Divisions was typical. They hammered at the western flank of the Jagst River Line and crossed it on April 5th and 6th, then battled furiously for four days before taking Jagstfeld, the town at the junction of Jagst and Neckar. One factory had to be shelled for an hour before it could finally be taken; the Americans found the mutilated bodies of fifty-eight SS men inside.

Meanwhile, at Heilbronn, the battle for the city was entering its final stage. On the morning of April 8th, armoured support at last reached the embattled troops on the southern bridgehead, over a treadway bridge which the engineers kept operating until noon when it was destroyed by enemy artillery. Shortly afterwards the two American bridgeheads joined up, and the Germans began to pull back. Heilbronn was finally occupied on April 12th, the Americans taking 1,500 prisoners.

During the week from April 13th-20th, the German First Army managed to retain a semblance of co-ordination among the fragmentary units extended along a line from the Löwenstein Hills to Nuremberg. Piecemeal and fluid as it was, this was nevertheless the only real front line left on the entire western front. It was defended by 15,000 troops, 20 artillery battalions and 100 tanks or self-propelled guns. On April 14th, there was no firm evidence of a carefully-laid German defensive plan; they did, however, appear to be withdrawing all their resources into the south-east of the country. It was therefore up to the Seventh Army to pierce the enemy line and frustrate any attempt by the retreating host to reach the sanctuary of the Austrian Alps.

The first of three crucial moves in the Allied plan was an attack on Nuremberg, which the Nazis had decided to defend to the last man as much for its associations with the Nazi Party as for any tactical reasons. Nuremberg represented the eastern anchor of the line still opposing the Seventh Army. It was a communications centre for the north-south railway system and the main highways, particularly those leading from Berlin to Munich, and—last but far from least in the eyes of the German leaders—it was the traditional shrine of the Nazi Party.

After XV Corps had reached the Höhe Rhon hill mass, it began to prepare immediately for the drive on Nuremberg, sending out reconnaissance probes south-eastward towards Bamberg and Coburg. These probes, carried out by the 106th Cavalry Group, were followed up by advance units of the 3rd and 45th Divisions, with flights of P-51 Mustang tactical reconnaissance aircraft sweeping the terrain ahead.

On April 12th, while the 106th Cavalry probed along the Nuremberg-Bayreuth autobahn, the 3rd and 45th Divisions moved up to take Bamberg. They met moderate fire from the town's defenders, but by April 13th they had cleared the whole of the town except for an island in the centre, formed by a circle of streams around marshy ground. The 180th Regiment crossed on a footbridge the next day and dislodged snipers who were still offering resistance. As soon as they knew they were completely cut off, the surviving Germans—some fifty men led by two officers—surrenderd and filed quietly into captivity across the bridge.

While Bamberg was under attack, other elements of both divisions drove a further 15 miles south-eastwards, and Combat Command B rejoined the 14th Armoured Division. After Bamberg fell, the 14th Armoured Division went on to cut the autobahn leading to Nuremberg, while the two infantry divisions approached the city on a broad front. The plan was to take Nuremberg in an enveloping movement. The 3rd Division on the right was to continue south-east, crossing the Regnitz River and the Ludwigs Canal, then strike south and clear that part of the city lying north of the Pegnitz River. The 45th Division was to advance further left, cross the Rednitz, and attack from the south and south-east. Elements of XXI Corps were to assist in the operation; the 14th Armoured Division and the 106th Cavalry were to undertake screening missions some miles out of the city.

By April 16th, the attacking divisions had formed a two-pronged pincer movement on Nuremberg, one having penetrated the northern outskirts and the other reaching the south-eastern suburbs. The garrison resisted fiercely; bitter fighting went on day and night, the enemy positions illuminated by American searchlight batteries. The city was ringed by 88mm flak guns, which wrought havoc among the American armour and infantry. As both US divisions broadened their fronts on April 17th, tightening the noose, the battle increased in intensity. XV Corps artillery supplemented the weapons of the two divisions, firing into the steadily decreasing target area, while fighter-bombers added their quota of firepower. By midnight on April 17th, the Americans had cleared nearly two-thirds of Nuremberg in bitter house-to-house combat.

The 1st Battalion of the 30th Infantry joined the fray on April 18th, attacking on the left. The next day they seized the north gate to the mediaeval walled city in the heart of Nuremberg, and held it as a bridgehead while the 2nd Battalion gained ground to the south. The remainder of the division fought its way through the smashed and burning streets towards the Pegnitz River, continually under the threat of attack from the rear by groups of enemy lurking in cellars and foxholes among the rubble. The 7th Infantry reached the inner city on April 19th; the 15th Infantry also attained this objective after fighting a bloody battle during which enemy civilians as well as troops hurled themselves against the American armour with small-arms, rifle grenades and Panzerfausts. The 45th Division in the south, which also reached the inner city on April 19th, met similar resistance.

On April 20th—Hitler's birthday—the murderous 88mm barrage died away as most of the enemy gun emplacements were overrun. At 1100, the 7th Infantry forced the walls of the inner city in its zone and began to push south, while the Germans started to surrender in large numbers to the 15th Infantry. At 1400 the 30th Infantry, with two battalions abreast, struck south and cleared the region north of the Pegnitz; at 1600 stronger opposition met the 45th Division coming up from the south, but this time the two assault regiments had eliminated all but 200 defenders who were barricaded in a tunnel. They were finally rooted out shortly before midnight.

The Gauleiter of Nuremberg, who had sworn to defend the Nazi Party bastion to the last and who had been awarded the Golden Cross of the German Order only hours before the collapse, was found dead in a cellar.

While the battle for Nuremberg was entering its last phase, another struggle was raging to the south-east at Stuttgart. With the Ruhr pocket now effectively reduced—it was declared annihilated the day before

Nuremberg fell—and with the Third Army drive approaching Salzburg, General Eisenhower had told General Devers on April 15th that the time was ripe for the Sixth Army Group to push south. The object would be to take Stuttgart and eliminate the German Nineteenth Army in the Black Forest. VI Corps, co-operating with the French, was to envelop Stuttgart, seize lines of communication between the city and the Swiss border, and exploit the situation as far as the frontier to cut off the Germans in the Black Forest while the French liquidated them.

Since April 13th, VI Corps had been driving south into the Löwenstein Hills. On the right flank, the enemy reacted sharply to the 100th Division's push towards Stuttgart, countering it savagely near Beilstein, 20 miles north of the city. The 3rd Battalion of the 399th Infantry approached a hill just north of Beilstein on the morning of April 18th; forward elements crossed the open draw below the hill, climbed its exposed northern slope and reached the wooded crest. The rest of the battalion was still climbing out of the draw when enemy mortars and artillery opened up on them, killing 17 GIs and wounding 101. When the battalion reached the crest, the Germans counter-attacked up the southern slope, suffering appalling casualties before they were finally driven off.

During the morning of April 19th, the advance of the 10th Armoured Division was delayed by steep hills and marshy valleys, but in the afternoon they made up for lost time by racing ahead for 17 miles. Combat Command A, carrying a power-saw to clear road-blocks, reached a cracking 40mph pace and seized a bridge over the River Rems at Lorch, driving into the town so swiftly that they captured the garrison—mostly bewildered Volksturm— almost without a shot being fired.

When elements of the 10th Armoured Division reached Kirchheim, they were within 15 miles of French forces which had advanced as far as Reutlingen. Stuttgart's fate was now virtually sealed; the enemy was left with only one escape corridor which was being progressively narrowed by the 100th and 103rd Divisions, pressing into it from the sides, and the enemy convoys were subjected to almost continual air attack. On April 22nd, the 100th Division took 1,000 prisoners in a pocket formed by the Neckar River north and east of Stuttgart and made contact with the French on the far bank. The 103rd met fiercer resistance on the 23rd in the hills to the north of the German escape route, but by nightfall the corridor had been sealed and the French armour was entering Stuttgart itself. French forces also drove into the Black Forest, mopping up pockets of Germans, while VI Corps veered south-east towards Ulm and the Danube in pursuit of the broken columns of the German Nineteenth Army.

In the centre of the Seventh Army front, the 4th and 42nd Divisions attacked in columns across the whole line of XXI Corps. On April 20th, the 12th Armoured Division probed out from Feuchtwangen towards the Danube, and in two days they covered 40 miles of ground to capture a 600ft bridge over the river at Dillingen. With the enemy's last line broken on both flanks and in the centre, the Seventh Army surged southwards on its next mission: to block the passes into Austria and seize the Innsbruck-Brenner Pass area. The German Nineteenth Army had been practically destroyed, while great gaps had been torn in the cohesion of their First and Seventh Armies by the relentless onsurge of the American armour. By April 25th, the US Seventh Army had taken, since the start of the invasion of southern France, the staggering total of 291,866 German prisoners. But the fight was not done yet. Ahead now lay the Danube, and the prospect of prolonged, fanatical resistance from men who had nothing more to lose.

Searching for snipers in the ruins of Waldenburg, VI Corps troops are pressing on towards Stuttgart on the right wing of the Seventh Army's thrust into Germany in April, 1945.

165

XII

By the time Nuremberg fell to the Seventh Army, it was clear that the war in Europe could not last much longer. The morale of the German High Command, and with it centralised combat leadership, was disintegrating rapidly. On the Seventh Army front, General Paul Hausser had been relieved from command of Army Group G, which had been virtually destroyed by General Patch's divisions on both sides of the Rhine. Remnants of more than a dozen enemy divisions were fleeing south with no co-ordinated orders; when they were told to make a stand, it was in positions that bore no semblance of a front line.

Meanwhile, General Patton's Third Army, which had been driving due east towards Prague and Dresden, began to alter course to move down the Danube for a junction with the Russians. Simultaneously, Patch started a Seventh Army swing towards the heart of Bavaria and the Tyrol. With General Brooks' VI Corps on the right, General Milburn's XXI Corps in the centre and General Haislip's XV Corps on the left, the Seventh Army was to stride quickly over the Danube and into the Bavarian foreland, making thrusts southward to cut the Alpine routes into the Inn River Valley and the Brenner Pass. The objective was to reduce the projected national redoubt of German last-line defence before it could be manned and organised. The Allies also hoped to uncover the concentration camps lying in the Seventh Army's path before the Nazis had a chance to liquidate their inmates and destroy evidence of their existence.

By April 21st, the Seventh Army had completed its turning movement for the coming campaign. Before it lay the Danube and the broad flats stretching away to the mountains. The main effort was on the right flank, and within forty-eight hours the breakthrough already achieved by VI Corps at Lorch was wildly accelerated, with two combat commands of the 10th Armoured Division racing ahead at speeds of up to 40mph. Behind the tanks, the 44th and 103rd Divisions strove to keep up the tempo, at the same time mopping up by-passed pockets of Germans. Opposition along the whole front was spasmodic and disorganised, although enemy battle groups still kept up their futile delaying tactics. The main obstacles were road-blocks and minefields, covered by small-arms fire. "Keep on going", General Brooks told General Morris, commanding the 10th Armoured Division. "Don't fight with them as there will be plenty of infantry behind you."

The tanks raced on for the Danube and all possible intact crossings between Ehingen and Ulm. This line seemed to be the next likely concentration point for what remained of General Foertsch's First Army, and the river itself was probably the best available position in the so-called final defence area on the north-western side of the redoubt.

The decision to attack Ulm involved a change of plan at Corps level. VI Corps turned south-east instead of south-west, a course of action dictated by the Stuttgart operation. The remnants of the German Nineteeth Army which had eluded the Stuttgart trap were fleeing south-eastwards, and the Seventh Army—notably the 100th and 103rd Divisions—moved in quickly to block the Kirchheim corridor and link up with the French.

On April 22nd, the Americans and the First French Army reached the Danube, and two days later two regiments of the 44th Division—with armoured support—struck out for Ulm. The city was strongly defended with artillery of all kinds, and the Germans held the east bank of the Iller River as far as its confluence with the Danube. Armoured elements succeeded in establishing a small bridgehead on the east bank, and troops of the 71st Infantry Regiment began to cross the river at this point on the evening of the 24th, moving out to take the defenders in the rear. The following morning, the Germans began to pull out, and were soon withdrawing in disorganised streams west of the river. Ulm itself, its mediaeval streets shattered by air attack, was occupied that afternoon.

The Danube River front in the Seventh Army zone wound its way north-east for some 80 miles from Ehingen to Neuburg, just west of Ingoldstadt, which fell to the Third Army on April 26th. By April 22nd, both the 10th and 12th Armoured Divisions had reached the Danube in the central sector, capturing the 600ft Dillingen bridge intact, and by early afternoon armoured spearheads had penetrated to within 20 miles of Augsburg. The 3rd Division was now called up from Nuremberg to take part in the pursuit. Allied air power had long since made enemy movements in daylight suicidal, so the Germans crossed the Danube during the nights of April 22nd and 24th. Their reaction to the American offensive was sharpest in the central sector; even the almost non-existent Luftwaffe threw in twenty or so fighter-bombers in eight sorties against the

Above: Troops of the 71st Infantry Regiment, 44th Division, cross the Danube unopposed near Berg during the Seventh Army's thrust to Ulm.

Below: Meeting no opposition, the 71st Infantry Regiment, 44th Division, cross the Danube in assault boats near Berg during the thrust towards Ulm.

Dillingen Bridge, while at Günzburg the 63rd Division—which had crossed the river without any supporting artillery—ran into stiff opposition, taking heavy casualties.

In the XV Corps sector, the 42nd and 45th Divisions also began their drive south-east to the Danube. For the most part, they encountered little resistance, although the enemy made an occasional stand; at Monheim, for example, there was a short, fierce battle when the Americans intercepted an armoured column. By April 25th, the divisions had closed the north bank of the Danube. The bridges across the river at Donauwörth were blown by the enemy only five minutes before the 42nd's tanks arrived. In the town itself, 700 defenders resisted desperately for six hours; the Americans took only sixteen prisoners. By midnight, the 45th Division—employing a non-stop shuttle service with high-powered motor boats—had deployed eight battalions across the river.

The Seventh Army had now completed its assault of the Danube, and XV Corps, like XXI and VI Corps on the right, was preparing for the drive across the Bavarian foreland to the mountains. The 20th Armoured Division replaced the 14th in XV Corps for the coming operation, and on April 27th the American armour moved over the river to advance on a broad front between the two major autobahns converging on Munich.

As soon as they received fresh stocks of gasoline, the bulk of VI Corps armour and infantry crossed the Danube and headed for the Tyrolean Alps and the Brenner Pass. They roared along at will, breaking apart the last remnants of General Brandenberg's Nineteenth Army. By April 26th, three columns were racing for the Memmengen-Mindelheim-Landsberg line, the speeding tanks festooned with infantry. As General Brooks said: "Push on and push hard . . . This is a pursuit, not an attack." At times the speed of the chase seemed unreal, with armoured units rolling on 30 miles in a day. Weakly-manned strongpoints were destroyed by mobile gunfire en route and huge enemy groups were rounded up and shipped to the rear. Armoured task forces wrought havoc with German columns and installations; one tank force ran across a large camouflaged airfield and destroyed a number of Messerschmitt 262 jets which were about to take off. More jet aircraft were found parked in makeshift dispersals among the trees at the side of an autobahn which had been used as a runway.

The assault sped through villages that, according to orders, were taken under fire unless white flags were displayed. The directive ran: "If you run into any resistance in the towns, particularly the big ones, I don't want you to take casualties. Use phosphorous, TDs and everything else and chew them to pieces." But the Americans did not encounter much resistance. On April 26th, the 411th Regiment of the 103rd Division entered

Landsberg; they met some sniper fire, but crossed the river the next morning to find a garrison of nearly 1,000 Hungarian troops all lined up to surrender formally.

Landsberg was another centre which had traditional significance for the Nazi Party. As they roved through the captured town, American troops added to their collection of war trophies a huge Swastika memorial flag and a bronze plaque which read: "Here a system without honour kept Germany's greatest son a prisoner from November 11th, 1923, to December 20th, 1924. In this cell Adolf Hitler wrote the book of the National Socialist Revolution *Mein Kampf.*"

The Americans soon came across one of the grim end-products of Hitler's 'struggle' when, on the road out of Landsberg, they overran a concentration camp. Some of the barracks had been set on fire, and charred corpses were strewn about. The GIs also discovered thousands of prisoners who were still alive crammed into huts; most of them were Jews, emaciated and in a state of almost complete physical and mental degeneration.

As the Americans drove for Memmengen, the Germans in the west found themselves under attack from three sides and resistance soon petered out. On the other bank of the Iller, tanks of Combat Command B came under heavy Panzerfaust and artillery fire and suffered some losses before the town was entered. German troops still held out in the hills around Memmengen, but made no attempt to launch a counter-attack; the Americans had already made it clear that in the event of any opposition they would destroy the town completely with artillery fire and air attack.

Seventh Army columns continued to the Landeck-Imst-Innsbruck line, bringing them closer to the Brenner Pass as they rolled through scattered resistance, by-passing pockets of enemy troops and burning vehicles. They were followed by the men of the 44th and 103rd Divisions, trudging along through rain and sleet. On April 29th, in the foothills of the Alps, the Seventh Army encountered some serious problems; General Patch's orders were to take Innsbruck with all possible speed, but this had little meaning as the Allied advance frequently became bogged down on the tortuous roads of the region—roads ready-made for enemy defensive points, strongly defended with artillery and antitank weapons. To make matters worse, elements of the 44th Division ran out of fuel. Armour and infantry were forced to move along the steep Alpine passes, constantly coping with craters, minefields, overturned vehicles, blown bridges and avalanches of rocks and snow created by the enemy.

Combat Command A, driving east, ran into a large crater completely blocking the road. A tankdozer filled it in and the column rolled on, only to find that a short distance beyond the enemy had blown a 50ft bridge over a gorge. This was by-passed by the tanks, which then ran into a mine belt, covered by sniper fire—with more blown bridges ahead. Meanwhile, Combat Command B was halted at a hairpin curve where a road-block of boulders, gravel and logs formed a barrier for 200 yards.

At this point, Seventh Army forces had already crossed into Austria. The 71st Infantry of the 44th Division captured Füssen on the River Lech, where the snow-fed torrent emerged through a gorge from the Austrian Tyrol. The blown bridge at Lech prompted a swing to the south-west over steep, wooded terrain to enter Austrian territory at Vils.

In the central sector of the Seventh Army's operations, American forces advanced on Augsburg. The city lay on the route of General Milburn's XXI Corps assault, and the 3rd Division was assigned to take it. The city stood at the confluence of the Lech and Wertach Rivers; it was dotted with canal spans and innumerable small bridges, which would have created real problems if they had all been blown by the Germans. However, the military importance of Augsburg was relatively slight; the large Messerschmitt factories in the southern suburbs had been demolished by Allied air raids, while the city was full of wounded German soliders in military hospitals.

As the Seventh Army approached Augsburg under cover of darkness, the forwards elements encountered some opposition from enemy road-blocks, but these were overwhelmed by the 12th Armoured Division. The next morning there was sporadic enemy shelling, but General O'Daniel of the 3rd Division gave orders to hold back counter-battery fire: "I don't want you to fire into Augsburg at all unless it is actually observed firing . . . Keep your eyes open for white flags or other signs of surrender as we have had many indications . . .''

Early on the morning of April 27th, 4th Division reported that two industrialists had come through to Burgau in an endeavour to capitulate and so spare Augsburg. Along the roads and in the fields, 88mm guns were found with white handkerchiefs and pillowcases fluttering from their barrels. A few German troops, however—numbering not more than 1,000—still hoped to hold the city; they had retreated all the way from the Danube and had received no orders to hold any other defensive line. As units of the 3rd US Division reached the outskirts of the city, alarm began to spread among the civilian population. Representatives of churches and commerce tried to prevail on General Fehn, the German commander, to surrender, and underground groups started to prepare for a coup. Fehn's garrison began to dwindle rapidly as men deserted, and by the morning of April 28th he had only eighty men under his command. The German 27th Artillery Replacement Regiment had melted away completely; road-blocks

Above: SS guards at Dachau concentration camp are subdued by liberating troops of the Seventh Army's 45th Infantry Division. The Germans on the ground are feigning death after the Americans had fired a volley after a fleeing SS man.

Below: An American soldier of the 45th Division hands out his few remaining cigarettes to inmates of Dachau concentration camp, liberated by the Seventh Army.

were unmanned; bridges had been only partly prepared for demolition. Nevertheless, General Fehn was a veteran army officer of forty-one years' service, and he had received no orders to surrender.

The US 3rd Division attacked in multiple columns. Colonel Edson, commanding the 15th Infantry, received word from his 1st Battalion as the US tank and infantry teams converged on the city in a sweeping arc: "Just got a phone call from Augsburg. People called the Freedom Party of Augsburg. Want to surrender the city. City in dissention . . ."

As the Americans drove through the suburbs the unrest came to a head. Underground groups banded together and improvised tactics; agents were sent around the city to spread rumours of surrender, telling people to fly white flags everywhere, while patrols went out to link up with the Americans. The 3rd Battalion commander was led up the street to the command post pillbox of General Fehn, who was given five minutes to surrender. The General made an abortive attempt to call up SS reinforcements on the telephone; by his side there was a sharp report as the deputy-Gauleiter of Augsburg shot himself. A moment later, the Americans forcibly removed the telephone from Fehn's hand and escorted him from the pillbox. A white flag fluttered from the tower of St Ulrich, the highest point in the city.

With resistance in Augsburg stifled before it had a chance to begin, American forces cut away to the east towards the Munich autobahn with orders to "barrel down the big highway". To the north of the autobahn, the Seventh Army flooded towards Munich itself. In the centre of XV Corps zone, the 42nd and 45th Divisions encountered a few delaying actions; ahead of them were the German 2nd Mountain Division and two SS Divisions, carrying out a skillful retreat.

Also ahead of the Americans lay Dachau, the first and largest concentration camp created by the Nazis. On the afternoon of Sunday, April 29th, when the first American soldier broke through the camp gates, Dachau contained more than 30,000 prisoners of every race, creed and political allegiance. I Company of the 222nd Regiment entered the camp at 1313 and the 2nd Battalion of the 157th Infantry at 1445, clearing it at 1705. General Linden, deputy commander of the 42nd Division, led the first forward patrol, and this is how he described what he saw:

"It was unbelievable. Freight cars full of piled cadavers no more than bones covered with skin, bloody heaps at the rail car doors where weakened prisoners, trying to get out, were machine-gunned to death by the SS . . . rooms stacked almost to the ceiling high with tangled human bodies adjoining the cremation furnaces . . . rooms where lay the dying survivors of the horror train, limp under filthy blankets, lying in human excreta, trying to salute our officers with broomstick arms, only to fall back . . .''

Some two weeks earlier, the Dachau commandant asked Himmler if the camp could be turned over to the Allies, but the request had been turned down. Instead, Himmler had ordered it to be evacuated at once. No prisoner was to be allowed to fall into Allied hands alive. Despite these orders, only one large-scale transport leaving Dachau had been organised before the Americans overran the area.

The 157th Regiment at this time was attacking past Dachau when a patrol stopped a German woman who was cycling north. She revealed that she had just come from Munich, crossing a bridge in the town of Dachau itself. Hearing about the bridge, Company L mounted tanks and raced for Dachau. The armoured column tore into the town; but, as the leading tank reached a point only 20 yards from the bridge, the enemy blew it up. A reconnaissance patrol quickly located a nearby footbridge and the Americans crossed it to assault the concentration camp, coming to the help of the US patrol already there. A stiff fire fight developed between the Americans and the SS guards, some 300 of whom were killed.

The prisoners went wild. Many rushed the electric fence surrounding the camp and died in the very hour of their salvation; others turned on their warders with savage fury, beating them to a pulp with fists and stones. SS men masquerading in prison clothing were hunted down and killed. The violence threatened to get out of hand, so eventually infantrymen had to fire over the inmates' heads to quieten them. The hysteria soon subsided. Flags and colours, improvised from sheets and scraps of cloth were raised throughout Dachau. Men sang the songs of their homelands; others danced; others wept. Yet others, their spirits broken by the long years of imprisonment, stood bewildered and petrified. Guarding the typhus-infested camp became a vital human and military duty. The combat troops moved out to take part in the four-division march on Munich, more than ever determined to wipe out the Nazis forever. The memory of Dachau would be with them for the rest of their lives.

The whole left flank of the Seventh Army was in motion for the drive on Germany's third largest city. With three-quarters of a million people, Munich ranked after Berlin and Hamburg; it was also the political, administrative and cultural centre of Bavaria. The US armour moved out in front during the night of April 27th/28th, closely followed by the motorised columns of the 42nd and 45th Divisions. After the capture of Augsburg, the 3rd Division used the autobahn and Highway 2 south of it, their columns driving through road-blocks and scattered German pockets.

The speed of the advance caused serious logistic problems; supply convoys simply could not keep up with it, and in the next few days transport aircraft flew 400,000 gallons of gasoline to forward airstrips to alleviate the worst shortages.

There was undeniable rivalry among the Seventh Army units for the prize of Munich. In Friedberg, east of Augsburg, General O'Daniel ordered his men to make maximum speed in the drive for the city. The rumour was that a Freedom Movement had developed there and that along the Augsburg-Munich autobahn only a handful of road-blocks and blown bridges barred the Americans' way. When news of the internal dissension in Munich reached the HQ of the 12th Armoured Division, a squadron of the 101st Cavalry Group was moved around the southern tip of the Ammersee and north-east up Highway 12 towards the city.

General White, the Army Chief of Staff, received a delegation from the city; they expressed a desire for it to be spared like Augsburg. Within the city, a limited civil war seemed to be brewing as the last days of April gave the anti-Nazi underground a chance for action. As the Seventh Army approached, various groups planned to strike against the Nazis; some of the effort was co-ordinated, but most was completely spontaneous.

The rebellion had a temporary success. The insurgents took the Nazi Governor of Bavaria, General Ritter von Epp, into custody, at the same time seizing the Munich radio station and converting it into a base for anti-Nazi propaganda. However, they failed to take the Party offices and army headquarters, and the revolt gradually began to lose ground. The signal had come too soon.

The half-encirclement of Munich by the 45th, 42nd and 3rd Divisions was almost complete on April 29th, although the city was not cleared until next day. Some time before noon on April 30th, forward troops of the 3rd and 42nd poured into the metropolitan area; they met no resistance and were greeted by groups of cheering civilians, waving white and Bavarian flags. The 45th met a less friendly reception from SS battalions in prepared defences centred around their college and barracks in the suburb known as the Hauptstadt der Bewegung. The Division had been moving forward with three regiments abreast. At 0630 on April 29th, the 180th Infantry followed the armour and attacked. Enemy fire at the railroad under-pass north of Oberschliessheim stopped the tanks, but this opposition was overwhelmed and the Americans began to cross the canal. The 179th Infantry, which had hacked its way to the Ingoldstadt-Munich autobahn, was also halted by artillery and small-arms fire, and bad weather prevented the use of air strikes to support ground forces.

The Division finally organised a three-pronged push into the heart of the city. The 157th Infantry attacked from Dachau at 0700 on April 30th, fighting its way through light opposition to reach the River Isar and secure the bridges. The 179th cleared Garching house by house and sped down into the city as far as the river. In the centre, the 180th still encountered savage SS resistance, but this was gradually snuffed out by barrages from 240mm howitzers. The infantry, however, was still compelled to advance under cover of smokescreens, and one battalion attacked and withdrew three times across open ground burning with 88mm, mortar and machine-gun fire. The purging of the SS college and barracks finally ended at 1500.

General Patch detailed the 45th Division to garrison the city, which had been turned into little more than a massive shell, and instructed XV Corps to prepare for further action after a two-day rest. VI Corps was faced with Innsbruck and Landeck, the Brenner and Resia Passes, while XXI Corps was about to enter the Inn River Valley.

As the last week of the European War opened, Seventh Army G-3 noted: "There is a growing need for maps of the Pacific area."

On May 1st, 1945, a mounting sense of excitement swept through the units of the Seventh Army, faced now with a confused and broken enemy force scattered between Innsbruck and Salzburg. General Foertsch's decimated First Army had no cohesion whatsoever; its ranks were reduced to less than 500 combat effectives. Only the SS, with some 7,000 troops, were still in a position to offer serious resistance. Further west, General Brandenberg's Nineteenth Army, with a strength of 3,000, had not a single division capable of effective defensive combat.

The enemy facing General Patch's triumphant forces, therefore, had neither an order of battle nor a front line. A top-secret telegram ordering the assumption of the Befehlshaber Nord command by General Jaschke marked the last instance of co-ordinated defensive instructions. Jaschke's primary task was to try to occupy the northern approaches to the Alpine frontiers and block the way into the mountains. Fortification of strongpoints was to be carried out with the utmost effort, using unarmed soldiers from disbanded units. However, very few of the Gauleiters to whom this directive was addressed ever received it. By May 2nd, the picture of overall collapse became even clearer; on this day the German forces in Italy surrendered, opening up the possibility of a link-up between the Fifth and Seventh US Armies.

The Seventh's next objective was the Inn Valley, isolated from Bavaria in the north and Italy in the south by two great ranges of precipitous mountains running roughly parallel north-east to south-west. Their walls were pierced by a number of roads leading to the watershed of the Inn River, flowing out of Switzerland through the heart of the Austrian Tyrol past Innsbruck. These roads scarcely formed suitable avenues of approach, as there were commanding heights ahead of them and on both flanks.

The unfavourable nature of the terrain brought a halt to the 10th Armoured Division's headlong dash; vehicles were caught up in bottlenecks, while the ground precluded the manoeuvres necessary for the proper use of armour. Infantry patrols alone managed to cope, and the 44th and 103rd Divisions pushed on towards the VI Corps objectives on the right flank: the passes leading into Austria. The almost vertical walls of the valleys, rising in forested slopes to the bare rock of the mountain peaks, crowded the invading troops into narrow corridors as they advanced. The few spring-like days of late April had now given way to a return of winter weather; snow and sleet fell, while heavy clouds filled the narrow valleys and canyons. To the west, the First French Army was fighting south into the Austrian province of Vorarlberg. The US 44th Divisions reached out towards the Fern and Resia passes, while the 103rd approached the Inn Valley through the Mittenwald Pass. To the south, the Fifth Army was advancing through the mountains of the southern Tyrol to join the Seventh Army.

For the infantry of the 44th, the first few days of May were spent in a series of stiff engagements for key mountain passes. The tortuous terrain made by-passing tactics impossible. German resistance focused on the Fern Pass, the better of the two leading into the Inn watershed. For forty-eight hours on May 1st and 2nd, the mountain crags reverberated to the crash of gunfire before the Americans overwhelmed enemy resistance with a well-executed envelopment of their rear, cutting the Germans off and enabling the American forces to link up for the final drive on Imst and Landeck.

For a day and a night, the 71st Infantry had made no progress against several hundred entrenched Germans using machine-guns, mortars and Panzerfausts, covering a series of craters on the road near Fern. One battalion fought past a landslide and a road-block to face the last holding force at the pass itself, while another battalion advancing in the rear was approached by a band of mountaineers. This party of five, an officer and four men of an Austrian partisan organisation, offered to guide the Americans over the mountains. There was apparently a little-known route to the east around the pass to Fernstein, lying just to the south at a point where a deep gorge was bridged. The Americans accepted the offer, and while the battle to the north continued they secured Fernstein, enabling elements to move up the highway and take the defenders in the rear.

On May 4th, the 44th Division cleared Imst and were in sight of Landeck. The troops moved in towards the little town of Mils, where the division fought its last battle. They left Mils burning and next day occupied Landeck, the troops anxiously awaiting news of a complete enemy surrender.

Further east on VI Corps front, meanwhile, the 103rd Division faced Innsbruck, the Seventh Army's main goal in the Tyrol. They were left in no doubt about their responsibility for penetrating the Inn Valley to the Brenner Pass. As General Brooks told General McAuliffe on May 1st: "All my chips are on you now. The other people have run into a 500ft chunk of blown road on the side of a cliff and it will particularly stymie them . . . so we have got to do it with you. So drive hard and toss your blocks out on all these roads that you pass."

By the end of the day, one regiment of the 103rd had rolled on beyond Mittenwald. Moving through Scharnitz earlier, divisional intelligence discovered that the local telephone exchange still had contact with enemy-held territory to the south; they at once put through a call and began to negotiate with the Innsbruck military command. However, during the four-hour period given to the Germans to consider the surrender demands, the lines went dead. There seemed good hopes of a truce, but when an enemy commander came forward under a white flag to propose an armistice pending negotiations, the US battalion commander refused the request. His orders were to continue the attack, and so fighting flared up once more around Seefeld and Reith.

Some time later, threats of immediate air and artillery bombardment of Innsbruck led to the desired agreement to surrender, and papers were prepared for the capitulation of the entire Tyrol-Vorarlberg area. Blindfolded American emissaries climbed 8 miles down the mountain from Reith into the Inn Valley. Members of the surrender party arrived at the agreed location only to find themselves taken prisoner—but then the German army negotiators were also seized and told that armed Austrians had taken over Innsbruck. That afternoon, the underground resistance had managed a successful coup; this complicated the issue somewhat for General McAuliffe, but on his own initiative he decided to call off the scheduled destruction of the town. On the evening of May 3rd, the Americans entered Innsbruck and accepted its formal surrender the next morning.

Also on the morning of the 3rd, the 409th Regiment of the 103rd Division was still battling on from Seefeld. The weather was icy as they entered Innsbruck with tank-mounted infantry at 1945, but the gloom was dispelled somewhat by cheering crowds waving the red and white banners

Above: Thrusting through Austria to secure the Brenner Pass, VI Corps infantry men are held up at Scharnitz by fanatical Nazi students. Under cover of the ditch and a tank destroyer, troops move cautiously into the town.

Below: Protected by a jeep and a tank, an infantryman doubles over to a better firing position at Scharnitz.

of the local partisans. The Americans, however, had no time to waste on liberation celebrations; the goal of VI Corps was still the Brenner Pass. That same night the 411th Regiment, fully motorised, moved out to race for the Italian border, its headlights blazing to lessen the hazards of the winding, icy roads. The 175-vehicle column raced on through freezing darkness, and at 0150 the leading units reached and took the pass. Later in the morning, at a point between Colle Isarco and Vipitèno in Italy, advance parties of General Patch's Seventh Army drove into units of General Truscott's Fifth Army, coming up from the south.

In the Inn Valley, an American mission was trying to get surrender negotiations under way with the enemy. At Hall, Major West, G-2 of the 3rd Division, located Gauleiter Hofer, Reichskommissar for the defence of the whole area and governor of Tyrol-Vorarlberg. Hofer confessed to the Americans that there were no longer organised bands of Wehrmacht or SS in the area, and that no defences existed between Innsbruck, Brenner and Salzburg. Only three of his own fifty-six battalions were left, and he was not in contact with them. Hofer denied that he had weapons in his home, but a search revealed three high-powered rifles with telescopic sights, three pistols and a short-wave radio. He was removed as a prisoner, and he bade goodbye to his household with a Nazi salute and a defiant 'Heil Hitler'.

After the Innsbruck incident, the surrender of the German forces in western Austria went off without a hitch. There was to be a motor escort, a guard with flags and colours, and a time schedule calling for all personnel to be at their posts by 1150 on May 5th in readiness for the arrival of the German commander at noon. No salutes were to be exchanged, nor any handshakes.

After a few formal objections, General Brandenberg was finally ready to sign the surrender documents at 1500 on May 5th. The American commanders present included Generals Brooks, McAuliffe, Morris and Dean. The unconditional surrender was accepted, and for the United States VI Corps and the First French Army, the war was over. According to the Innsbruck surrender terms, all forces including para-military units would cease all acts of hostility towards forces of the United Nations not later than 1800 on May 5th, 1945. The Germans were to disarm themselves and remain in their positions until their arms were collected; they were also required to provide a detailed troop list and a catalogue of minefields. Orders for surrendering prisoners-of-war, political prisoners, hostages and deportees were to be complied with at once. The Germans were strictly prohibited from wearing or displaying Nazi Party badges, brassards, flags or decorations.

Meanwhile, in the centre of the Seventh Army front, General Milburn's

Above: For the German soldiers waving a white flag the war is over. It is almost over too for the Seventh Army, the XV Corps of which is here seen entering Berchtesgaden below Hitler's hilltop home.

Below: Götterdämmerung—Hitler's mountain home blazes, fired by the SS troops guarding it as the Seventh Army enter Berchtesgaden on 4th May, 1945.

XXI Corps was attacking towards the north-west. These central forces were denied easy access to the Inn Valley by rugged mountains running parallel with the river. While the 36th and 4th Divisions struck directly at the valley, the 12th Armoured Division circled eastwards to search for natural access points.

This swing in the centre tended to unbalance the offensive; XXI Corps pushed over on the line of XV Corps, which was now no longer facing south but pointing towards the Salzburg Gap. The city of Salzburg lay in the Third Army zone, and Patton was not prepared to advance on the Salzach River corridor until he had enough infantry to support his armour. The fear was that German troops, fleeing in front of the Third Army, might pour through the Salzburg Pass into the 'Alpine Redoubt' region. The zones were quickly switched, and the Seventh Army was assigned the task of striking into Salzburg.

The drive began on the afternoon of May 2nd, the Americans brushing aside light resistance—mainly from boys—in wooded areas. They accepted the surrender of the Rosenheim garrison, although one enemy colonel threatened to resist in his poison-gas dump area unless he was given twenty-four hours to evacuate. The Americans advanced regardless of this threat, and in the early evening of May 2nd the 106th Cavalry Group took the surrender of General Ferenc-Loszak together with 8,000 officers and men of the Hungarian Army.

All along the route of the Seventh Army attack, villages and towns flew white flags; any that failed to do so needed only a few bursts of machine-gun fire to prompt a sudden display. Task forces chased the disintegrating enemy so rapidly that they sometimes found themselves isolated; and behind them, hour by hour, the main roads became increasingly choked by the mass of surrendering German formations and their straggling columns of motor and horse-drawn vehicles.

American armour and infantry were striking freely in every sector of the mountain area. The 103rd Division, aiming for Innsbruck and the Brenner Pass, sent a detachment 30 miles down the Inn Valley to contact XXI Corps. XV Corps, with the 20th Armoured supporting the 3rd, 42nd and 86th Divisions, swept on towards the Salzach.

The attack on the city of Salzburg was less of a combat manoeuvre than a giant motorcade. The prize was not only the city but Berchtesgaden, Hitler's retreat lying in the shadow of the Obersalzberg mountain. Virtually no resistance hindered the advance now, and the long lanes of the autobahn, conceived as strategic roads to facilitate German military manoeuvres, served the Americans well. The Germans were without transport, armour or artillery; only a few paltry rounds of small-arms

Top: Hitler's mountain home on fire 4th May, 1945.

Above: Seventh Army troops tear down the Nazi flag.

crackled out from the occasional road-block. The American divisions had seized everything on wheels, including all the trucks of their now unemployed supporting artillery battalions.

They met no trouble at Salzburg. The town was being shelled when the garrison commander sent out a delegation to offer unconditional surrender on the morning of May 4th. This was accepted by General O'Daniel under a sky still blanketed by post-seasonal snow, as a cold, damp wind whipped across the highways from the Tyrolean Alps.

After the surrender, XV Corps hooked back into Germany through the Salzburg Pass towards Berchtesgaden, some 10-15 miles to the south-west. General Milburn had already committed elements of the 101st Airborne Division and General Leclerc's 2nd French Armoured Division—which had rejoined the Seventh Army for its final drive after operations against the German pockets on the Atlantic coast—to a XXI Corps thrust towards Hitler's mountain eyrie. During the night of May 3rd/4th, however, General Patch, cutting in on a telephone conversation between Generals Haislip and O'Daniel, found that the immediate capture of Berchtesgaden was feasible, so he assigned the task to the 3rd Division. Personnel at the new Seventh Army command post, which had opened in Augsburg at noon on May 3rd, watched the 3rd's progress—the last advance undertaken by the Division of their Odyssey from the beginning of Operation 'Dragoon' to the final victory in Europe.

Early in the afternoon of May 4th, elements of the 3rd Division were reported about 2½ miles from Berchtesgaden. The Obersalzberg mountain was still smouldering from the effects of Allied bombing during April, and from local fires started by desperate SS guards. Motorised task forces wound their way up to the mountain hideout and entered it at precisely 1558 hours on May 4th. The 7th Regiment arrived after dark, followed by the rest of the 3rd Division, French armour and patrols of the 101st Airborne. The next morning, American troops tore down the Nazi banners and raised the US flag.

It was almost the last act; almost, but not quite. After the capitulation in Italy, Field-Marshal Kesselring had asked General Wolff, commanding the SS in northern Italy, to find out whom he should approach regarding his own surrender. SHAEF informed General Devers of Kesselring's request and the German High Command HQ were told that a conference would be arranged with representatives of Sixth Army Group.

Seventh Army units in the Salzburg sector were alerted for the approach of the Kesselring party, which would arrive in a vehicle with a white covering over the hood and bearing a white flag. During the night of May 4th/5th, the 3rd Infantry Division made contact with the surrender

Above: A tank loaded with infantrymen of the XV Corps, Seventh Army, rolls into Berchtesgaden. In the background are the snow-covered alps where remnants of the German Army made their last stand.

Below: Where armies meet—near Nauders on the Austrian-Italian border, 7th May, 1945. The men striding down the road have come by way of Sicily, France, Germany and Austria with the Seventh Army. They are greeted by men of the Fifth Army who have fought their way up through Italy.

delegation headed by General Foertsch, acting for General Schultz of Army Group B. The Americans escorted them to a large estate near Munich, where, on a grey, rainy Saturday morning, the terms of unconditional surrender for the German armies on the southern front were dictated.

The Thorak Estate at Haar was a formidable grey stone structure with granite steps, marble floors and massive doors and windows, its large rooms crowded with statues. The Germans had their own conference room on one side; on the other, at the far end of the table and facing the door, General Devers waited with Generals Patch and Haislip and their staffs. The two parties had already met in the courtyard; no salutes were exchanged. Lieutenant-Colonel Hentry Cabot Lodge, of Sixth Army Group, recorded the meeting:

"General Foertsch mounted the few polished black marble steps and stood in the open door. He wore the polished black boots and light field-grey uniform of the German Army. Around his neck was the Iron Cross . . . He was followed by the officers of his party, similarly dressed, although with less ornamentation . . . General Menoher (XV Corps Chief of Staff) presented General Foertsch to General Devers and General Foertsch in turn presented his officers, each of whom stood and bowed when his name was called . . .

"General Foertsch began to speak, taking up the paragraphs of the surrender document one by one. He spoke in a clear, deep voice, very slowly and distinctly, so that every word could be understood by anyone having even a smattering of German. He never argued. He knew, of course, that he was beaten. He would often begin his statements with the sentence: 'I deem it my duty to point out . . .' and then would show, for example, that the German troops were so scattered that it would take more than the contemplated number of hours to get the news to them. Or else, coming to the dumps of German weapons which were to be established, he asked that they be guarded by armed men, lest disorderly elements in the country steal the weapons and thereby threaten law and order. He hoped that officers and military police could keep side-arms in order to maintain tranquility. His suggestions were all of that type. He stressed the number of refugees and the lack of food in his area.

"General Devers would respond, asking questions and giving his views. After brief discussions, each point in turn was taken up. Boundaries were settled, the time schedule was established on the big points. There was to be no 'armistice'; this was unconditional surrender . . ."

The point had to be made quite clear. At the will of the Allies, all personnel of Army Group G, including Foertsch and Schulz, would become prisoners-of-war. Foertsch sat stiffly to attention. A full minute passed before he said anything. He was clearly suffering from violent emotion. Finally he broke the silence, bowed his head slightly, flushed a little, and replied: "I understand. I have no choice. I have no power to do otherwise . . ."

The meeting was adjourned at 1430. An hour or so later, the surrender was complete with the signatures of Devers, Foertsch, Patch and Haislip. As from noon on May 6th, all German forces under the command of Army Group G were to cease all acts of hostility towards the United Nations. All enemy elements were to disarm themselves at once, and remain in their positions. The German Army relinquished nearly 100,000 square miles of territory, south of the Allied lines to the Swiss and Italian borders, and from the Rhine eastward to about 20 miles beyond Salzburg.

The SS, however, considered itself divorced from any commitments made in its name by Foertsch, and representatives of Army Group G passing back to their own lines after the surrender could expect no safe conduct from their more fanatical compatriots. SS patrols blew a crater in front of the delegation's vehicle, and set up two road-blocks behind it. Foertsch went on ahead by himself and managed to get through, but the others turned back to the 3rd Division command post, which they reached in the middle of the night of May 6th/7th.

In the meantime, high in the mountains, some enemy troops surrendered and others elected to fight on, while in a castle near Woergl a minor war broke out. The Itter castle, standing on a high knoll, was the prison of Edouard Deladier and Paul Reynard, former premiers of France; Generals Maurice Gamelin and Maxim Weygand; a sister of General de Gaulle and a son of Georges Clemenceau. The SS garrison resisted fiercely as the Allies tried to occupy the place, and within the castle walls American and German troops fought side by side to eliminate them.

Berchtesgaden had been reached and the war was over at last, but the Seventh Army had one more job to do. During the eventful four days of May 5th, 6th, 7th and 8th, the Americans turned their attention to personalities in their sectors to be liberated, like the French in Itter Castle. They also stretched a dragnet across southern Germany to trap prominent Nazis.

By May 8th, Generals von Rundstedt, von Leeb and von List had already been seized by Seventh Army men. On the 7th, the 106th Cavalry Group sent out patrols to the east from Salzburg, and in a villa near the village of Strobl troops found King Leopold of Belgium under guard. The guards offered no resistance, and Leopold was quickly set free.

The hunt went on for Reichsmarschall Hermann Göring, and Baron Oshina and his Japanese Embassy staff. There was also a systematic search for the looted treasures of art, gold and jewels which the Germans had hidden away in the Tyrol. The Americans suddenly stumbled on a staggering fortune in oriental rugs, oil paintings, tapestries and cases of gold and diamonds in twenty-five Hungarian freight cars, shunted into a mountain siding.

Cavalry patrols combed the mountains, ferreting out high-ranking German officers. Field-Marshal Kesselring turned up at the headquarters of the 101st Airborne Division, where he made it clear that he could not be expected to hold conferences with a mere local Allied commander. Through 3rd Division communications facilities, he announced himself to the Supreme Allied Commander as Commander-in-Chief West and Feldmarshall of the Southern District. He was arrested.

On the very morning of VE Day, May 8th, Colonel von Brauchitsch, Göring's aide de camp, presented two letters from the former Luftwaffe chief to the Allied command post in Kufstein. These contained offers of surrender, coupled with pleas to the Supreme Commander for an interview so that they could talk "as one soldier to another".

The word went out to pick up Göring. He was not in his castle, which was guarded by fully armed SS troops of the Florian Geyer Division, but Brigadier-General R. I. Stack, of the 36th Division, found the whole Göring entourage parked along the road a few miles from Radstadt in Austria. As the German party was escorted to the American lines, one of the SS officers became unmanageable and had to be shot, although Göring himself was affable enough. Yet there was no forgetting his part in the most cruel war in history; a war that had cost the Seventh Army alone, between August, 1944 and May, 1945, 15,271 dead and 58,342 wounded.

On Thursday, May 10th, 1945, General Patch issued an order of the day to his troops. It ended with these words: "To you who have done the fighting I send my deepest and most patriotic thanks."

They knew that it was no idle tribute; for Patch, along with the officers and enlisted men who had survived the bloody months of conflict, had lived the Seventh Army's story to the end.

Index

189

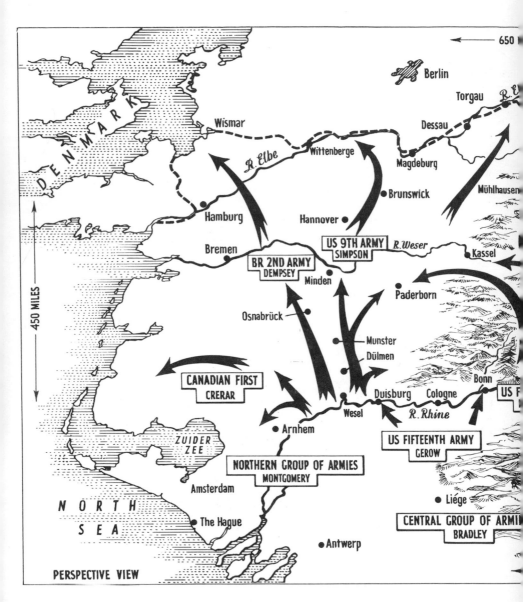

Berlin

Torgau   R. E

Dessau

Wismar

Magdeburg

D E N M A R K   R. Elbe   Wittenberge

Brunswick   Mühlhausen

Hamburg   Hannover

US 9TH ARMY
SIMPSON   R. Weser

Bremen   Kassel

BR 2ND ARMY
DEMPSEY   Minden

450 MILES   Paderborn

Osnabrück

Munster

Dülmen

CANADIAN FIRST
CRERAR   Bonn

Duisburg   Cologne   US F

Wesel   R. Rhine

ZUIDER
ZEE   Arnhem

US FIFTEENTH ARMY
GEROW

Amsterdam

NORTHERN GROUP OF ARMIES
MONTGOMERY

N O R T H   Liége

S E A   The Hague

CENTRAL GROUP OF ARMI
BRADLEY

Antwerp

PERSPECTIVE VIEW

BATTLE OF GERMANY